Kokopelli

Kokopelli

The Making of an Icon

Ekkehart Malotki

University of Nebraska Press

Lincoln and London

Publication of this volume was assisted by The Virginia Faulkner Fund,
established in memory of Virginia Faulkner,
editor-in-chief of the University of Nebraska Press.

Library of Congress Cataloging-in-Publication Data

Malotki, Ekkehart.
Kokopelli : the making of an icon / Ekkehart Malotki.
p.   cm.
Includes bibliographical references and index.
ISBN 0-8032-3213-6 (cloth : alk. paper)
1. Kokopelli (Pueblo deity) I. Title.

E99.P9 M225 2000
979—dc21
99-088276

To Pat McCreery—a true friend, with a heart and mind for rock art.

Contents

Illustrations

Preface

The idea for this book was first conceived on a hot July evening in 1989, following a campfire talk in Utah's Canyonlands National Monument. Some of the details of that evening I remember very vividly. At one point in the informal program, the seasonal ranger in charge asked her audience to identify a number of rock art symbols that she had drawn on some pieces of cardboard. When she held up the generic figure of a humpbacked fluteplayer, the assembled visitors, almost in unison, responded "Kokopelli."

This intrigued me, for "Kokopelli" resembled the Hopi pronunciation of Kookopölö, a kachina; and in all the years I had visited the Hopi reservation I had never observed, during numerous plaza or night dances, a Kookopölö kachina, either male or female, with a flute. Nor had such a connection of this musical instrument with the kachina ever been mentioned in the context of any of the narratives or ethnographic lore that I had recorded during nearly sixteen years of scholarly work on the preservation of Hopi oral traditions. In fact, the only connection between the kachina and the fluteplayer image is that "Kokopelli" is a phonetic approximation of the kachina's name.

The current popularity of Kokopelli is based on a misunderstanding. I felt like pointing this out to the group but then reconsidered, for cultural misassociations such as the fluteplayer with the Hopi kachina and linguistic corruptions such as "Kokopelli" for "Kookopölö" are, after all, normal and universal processes in the history of contact between cultures. To regret or condemn these misassociations and corruptions would be inappropriate, since present-day American and Hopi cultures are in part the products of similar misassociations and corruptions over the millennia.

That night around the campfire, the term "Kokopelli" flourished for the rest of the session. Indeed, before long, a veritable brainstorming discussion was under way, with everyone attempting to outdo each other in suggesting a more convincing *raison d'être* for Kokopelli's depiction as a fluteplayer in the stony annals of the Colorado Plateau.

One of the participants even alluded to the supposed South American origin of the figure. He may have been familiar with the work of Hugh Cutler

(1944: 290–94), who theorizes that "Kocopelli of the Utah and Arizona canyons" may have been a remote ancestor of the flute-playing Callahuayo Indians of Bolivia. According to him, many of these Indians, in their role as nomadic medicine men, journey not only about their Andean home territory but all over South America and even to Central America. Since pod corn tucked away in their blanket backpacks is still part of their stock in trade, he argues that it is possible one of their ancestors, "similarly equipped, carried pod corn to North America and became the legendary flute player, Kocopelli."

Intrigued by the lively debate, I decided to conduct a probe of my own into the Kokopelli phenomenon, which, though it had not yet reached the current marketing frenzy, was swiftly gaining in popularity.

The decision to examine the identification of Kookopölö the Hopi kachina deity with Kokopelli the petroglyphic or pictographic fluteplayer and to try to clear up this confusion using reliable ethnographic material came naturally to me. On the one hand, I was developing an ever-deeper interest in the rock art of the American Southwest, its iconography, its cultural functions as a subject of speculation in the borderland between archaeological evidence and ethnographic description of more recent cultures, and its strange but powerful aesthetics (see McCreery and Malotki 1994). Even more important was my ongoing study of the Hopi language of today and the way it affects and is affected by the cultural order and belief system of this Pueblo people. This scholarly occupation had led me to collect not only linguistic data but also a wealth of cultural information contained in Hopi oral tradition. My familiarity with the language and the culture made me aware of the numerous scholarly and popular myths about the Hopi, ranging from Benjamin Lee Whorf's epochal yet erroneous claim that the Hopi language contains no reference to time (see my refutation in Malotki 1983a) to the association of the term "Hopi" with "peaceful" (Malotki 1991: 45–46). Transcultural insights can never be entirely reliable since they are tinged by the culturally preconditioned biases of the observer. Any endeavor to appraise the natural phenomena, artifacts, practices, ideas, and beliefs of a given culture as accurately as possible requires careful attention to the lexical thesaurus that a particular speech community has to offer.

For these reasons, I decided that the main body of evidence required to dissociate the kachina Kookopölö from the rock art symbol of the fluteplayer had to be grounded in Hopi-based ethnography. I had already accumulated much of the Hopi cultural information pertinent to the issue between the late 1970s and the mid-1980s. By that time, proficiency in spoken Hopi had already started to deteriorate among the younger Hopi generation, taking with it all the cultural treasures that are anchored in a people's own vernacular.

For the purpose of preservation, I had collected hundreds of tales, legends, and myths, primarily from story "rememberers," as I prefer to characterize them. Most of the rememberers were speakers of the Hotevilla dialect of Third Mesa; however, Hopis from the First Mesa village of Walpi and the Second Mesa communities of Shungopavi and Shipaulovi also contributed to my corpus of narrative materials. Along with the tales, I collected any and all ethnographic information that was volunteered to me, ranging from terms for cat's cradle figures to beliefs surrounding the supreme god, Maasaw, from songs of every kind (with the exception of love songs, which are completely absent from Hopi culture) to native food recipes, from old-time children's games to the constantly growing body of Hopi prophecies.

In the summer of 1989, when I took stock of the materials relevant to this project, I found that I was in possession of three Kookopölö stories and three Cicada tales. I also had a wide array of ethnographically solid folk statements that shed light on the central figures of this case of cultural confusion: the male god Kookopölö, his female counterpart Kokopölmana, and maahu, "the cicada," which appears to be the underlying insect model for the fluteplayer in rock art imagery. While most of these ethnographic data had been recorded spontaneously, I set out to make inquiries in a more systematic fashion about the various aspects of these three evolving players in the Kokopelli drama. To some extent, I did this by drawing on all the available English sources in an attempt to verify or refute them in the field. This approach yielded many new and often unexpected insights into the roles of the two kachina deities and the insect in Hopi culture.

This book—the result of that approach—begins with a preliminary investigation into the phenomenon of Kokopelli and its relation to the Hopi kachina Kookopölö. Part 1 then analyzes the ethnographic elements of the Kokopelli phenomenon, including Kookopölö, his female counterpart Kokopölmana,

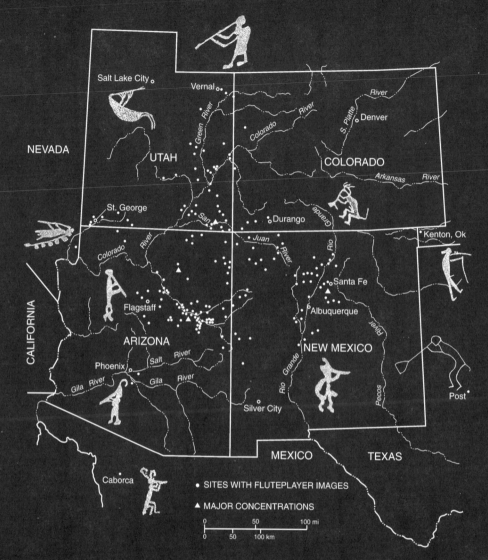

Figure 1: Fluteplayer distribution

Fluteplayer images, in the form of petroglyphs and pictographs on rock faces, are widely dispersed over the Colorado Plateau and adjacent regions. The images, manufactured over a long period of time from as early as A.D. 800 to historic times, reflect a wide variety of morphologies and associations undoubtedly related to the developing cultural functions of the fluteplayer personage in Native American societies. Major image concentrations occur at sites along the San Juan River in southeast Utah, in the Rio Grande Valley in north-central New Mexico, south of Black Mesa in northeastern Arizona, and along the Little Colorado River in east-central Arizona. Fluteplayer images on the periphery, illustrated here, are generally solitary, isolated and relatively simple in design, but show considerable variation from one peripheral region to the next.

and the cicada, the figure associated with the fluteplayer, in the light of the ethnographic material I have been able to collect. Part 2 presents six Hopi oral tales in an effort to show the contrast between authentic Hopi traditional material and the formation of the Kokopelli icon.

For reasons of linguistic preservation as well as cultural authenticity and sensitivity, the ethnographic texts in this work are presented bilingually. Constituting original Hopi source material, they owe their existence to the remarkable memory of several Hopis from Third, Second, and First Mesa who were strongly interested in seeing significant portions of their cultural heritage preserved for posterity. Although the ethnographic texts and the tales complement each other in establishing a clear borderline between the domain of Kookopölö and that of the cicada, the corpus of ethnographic texts with its numerous analytic details must be considered primary. Since, with the exception of "The Boy Who Went in Search of the Cicadas," the tales have all previously appeared in bilingual story collections of mine (Malotki 1995 and 1998), the original Hopi versions are omitted here.

Regrettably, with the exception of Lorena Lomatuway'ma, all of the Hopi contributors to this book are deceased. My utmost gratitude goes to the late Michael Lomatuway'ma, my friend and collaborator of many years. In the early and mid-eighties, when I amassed the bulk of my Hopi oral literature, his contributions were extensive. Two of the six stories preserved in this book, "The Long Kwasi of Kookopölö" and "The Cicadas and the Serpents," are his.

The English renderings of the Kookopölö and Cicada stories, as well as of the ethnographic passages, are mine. I tried to steer a middle course between too close and too free a translation. Michael's wife, Lorena, greatly assisted me during the lengthy translation process undertaken several years after Michael's untimely death in 1987. I consulted her in all instances where I had translation difficulties. For any errors or other shortcomings in the final English versions, however, I alone am accountable.

Lorena, initiate of the Maraw women's society at Hotevilla, also narrated three of the tales contained in this volume: "The Man-Crazed Woman," "The Orphan Boy and His Wife," and "The Crying Cicada." In addition, a good portion of the ethnographic details is hers. Also, since her mother, Rebecca, was present during many of our working sessions, Lorena frequently elicited precious ethnographic facts from her, which she then dictated to me. Her wonderful command of the wealth of her native language and her intimate familiarity with all aspects of Hopi culture eminently qualified her to assist me in the final preparation of this book. Lorena's enthusiastic and formidable contribution is therefore acknowledged with a great sense of obligation and gratitude.

"The Boy Who Went in Search of the Cicadas," finally, was obtained from a Walpi man from First Mesa. It was his wish to remain anonymous, just as it was the choice of a Second Mesa man from Shungopavi who shared an immense amount of cultural lore with me in the course of several years. This person was endowed with a near-encyclopedic knowledge of Hopi culture, and his death was not only a great loss for Hopi scholarship but an immensely greater one for the Hopi community at large.

As has been the case with the majority of my other publications, the English prose style of this manuscript was greatly improved by the editorial skills of Ken Gary. While all of his editing suggestions were thankfully accepted, I am most grateful to Ken for effecting a thorough metamorphosis of my prefatory and introductory materials. He was supported in this effort by valuable suggestions from William Bright and Helmbrecht Breinig. In addition, Helmbrecht Breinig left his imprint on the conclusion, aided in part by Ken Gary and Don Weaver. Don, who heads his own archaeological company in Flagstaff, also agreed to collaborate on the captions for the black-and-white illustrations and the photos. It is the purpose of these captions to complement the essentially ethnographic nature of this work with a series of archaeological conclusions that he drew from his professional expertise regarding the fluteplayer symbol in Southwestern rock art imagery. Don's findings are based primarily on the recording of the extensive Taawa site on the Hopi reservation, whose inventory of more than 12,000 rock art glyphs contains some 175 fluteplayers, making it the site with the highest density of fluteplayer icons anywhere in the Southwest. Ken Gary, finally, needs to be acknowledged here once more for rising to the challenge of creating an index for this work.

For the preparation of the attractive illustrations I thank Dolber Spalding. Her care and skill in completing this task was most impressive.

Several other individuals contributed significantly to this work: Pat McCreery, with whom I coauthored Tapamveni: The Rock Art Galleries of

Petrified Forest and Beyond, first introduced me to the rock art theater of Petrified Forest and provided a multitude of leads to fluteplayer sites. Jim Duffield, endowed with a sixth sense for tracking down fluteplayers, accompanied me to a number of sites in the Rio Grande area of New Mexico and other regions of the American Southwest. My son, Patrick, sharing my rock art enthusiasm in the wild, as always, needed little prompting to tackle photographic challenges that required climbing ability and a lack of acrophobia.

I would also like to express my sincere gratitude to Henry Hooper. In his capacity as Associate Vice President for Research and Graduate Studies at Northern Arizona University, he strongly supported this project and approved camera-ready production of the manuscript. Execution of this task was performed with great expertise by Louella Holter, editor at the Ralph M. Bilby Research Center. Daniel Boone, imaging specialist at NAU's Bilby Research Center, was in charge of all technical aspects concerning the artwork. To both I owe a very special thanks.

To William Bright and Jerry Brody I am most grateful for their enthusiastic endorsement of the work to the University of Nebraska Press. I also need to mention Stephen Barnett, my copyeditor, who did an outstanding job shaping the final version of the manuscript.

Finally, there is a large number of people, many of them rock art aficionados, to whom I am indebted for sharing, over the years, their fluteplayer images in the form of drawings or photos or for responding to my occasional Internet inquiries or other information requests: Jean Allan, Mary Allen, George Baker, Jack Beckman, Alain Briot, Deborah Bouldin, Jerry Brody, Grace Burkholder, Jeff Burton, Robert Carter, Gilbert Campbell, Lou Cawley, Sally Cole, Helen Crotty, John V. Davis, Claire Dean, Allen Dearwester, Ike Eastvold, Gene Foushee, Stew Fritts, Phil Geib, Christine Gralapp, Bill Heidrick, Winston Hurst, John Irwin, Glenn Kearsley, Don Keller, John A. Labadie, Edmund Ladd, Robert Mark, Leigh Marymor, Daniel McCarthy, Terry Moore, Breen Murray, Joe Orr, Joe Pachak, John Parsons, Richard Payne, Alex Patterson, Peter Pilles, Peter Price, Pete Rhode, Rebecca Roush, Eric Ritter, Curtis and Polly Schaafsma, Emory Sekaquaptewa, Albert Snow, Dennis Slifer, Ernie Snyder, Edward Stasack, Kitty Stoddart, Kay Sutherland, Dennis Tedlock, Shelby Tisdale, Solveig Turpin, Wilson Turner, Sharon Urban, Jesse Warner,

Katherine Wells, and John Young. Evelyn Billo graciously shared a fluteplayer slide (Plate 9) for inclusion in my selection of color photographs. My profound apologies to anyone who feels he or she should have been included in this list but whose name I failed to mention.

Introduction
The Kokopelli Phenomenon

Probably no other image in the entire body of Southwestern iconography has attracted as much attention as that of the fluteplayer. This seems to be true both in ancient as well as modern times. The anthropomorphic fluteplayer must have intrigued the minds of various prehistoric cultures, since he occurs within a large geographic region of the Four Corner states and is distinguished by a high degree of cultural longevity. Besides the fluteplayer's primary manifestation in rock art, that is, in petroglyphs and pictographs, the icon is a frequent design element on precontact ceramic ware. Lambert (1967: 398) also reports a clay effigy vessel in his likeness, and Carr (1979: 13) claims his existence in "the kiva mural art of the Pueblos" but presents no pictorial evidence.

Yet the prehistoric interest in the flute-playing image is nothing compared to its ubiquity and near-obsessive fascination in today's mainstream American culture. Known as Kokopelli, the fluteplayer lends its image to a vast range of twentieth-century institutions, from cafes and restaurants to miniature golf courses, from bicycle trails to chamber quartets. Its apparent charm has inspired names for "motels and stores, galleries, nightclubs, realty offices, rafting companies and recorder societies" (Slifer and Duffield 1994: 139).

The classic portrayal of Kokopelli is often endowed with a hump and a phallus in addition to the flute. However, it is the depiction of a sticklike flutist with an arched back, whose prototype is found on Hohokam red-on-buff pottery fragments from southern Arizona dated about A.D. 1000, that has gained the most widespread use in today's popular culture. The reason for this predilection appears obvious: it is "safe," for it lacks the exposed genitals.

This Hohokam-derived image and the figure in other postures, occasionally even with the addition of an erect penis, are encountered as a decoration on a nearly limitless array of knick-knacks, tourist souvenirs, and other gadgets. This pan-Southwestern icon appears on the letterheads of stationery, business cards, raffle tickets, T-shirts, street signs, freeway underpasses, posters and advertisements for jazz fests, and even AIDS conferences, to name but a few examples. Kokopelli's portrait is ever-present in contemporary Native

American arts and crafts, comprising such media as jewelry, ceramics, textiles, and paintings, and it is a mainstay in the assortment of wrought iron and steel cutouts that fill the shelves of curio stores or adorn the patios and lawns of southwestern-style residences.

This total commoditization has led to increasingly outlandish manifestations of the Kokopelli motif in mail order catalogs and even on the Internet, where it is intended to reach the widest possible audience of mainstream America. In the *Wireless Holiday II 1995* catalog, for instance, published by Minnesota Public Radio, "Golfer-Pelli," a steel figure of Kokopelli swinging a golf club, takes his place alongside such items as the Classic Beer Guide poster, Snoopy and Felix the Cat pet dishes, and the Swiss Army Cavalry watch. Helpfully, the blurb for Golfer-Pelli states that "it is believed that Kokopelli could make the wind talk and call the clouds; perhaps Golfer-Pelli can improve your swing!" Not content with golfing, the World Wide Web site for the Pelli-People also offers his image in such roles as scuba diver, rock guitarist, and skateboarder. The *New Mexico Catalog* offers a wide range of Kokopelli household items such as andirons, light switch covers, lamps, and mirrors ("Kokopelli on the wall, who's the fairest of them all?"). An insightful sampler of the ever-growing scope of Kokopelli applications is available in Walker (1998). His photographic survey portrays the icon in conjunction with cookies, welcome mats, money clips, Christmas ornaments, pantyhose, and even a street name, to mention but a few. It seems as if there is no limit to the ways in which the Kokopelli motif can be applied.

Kokopelli has also entered popular mainstream literature in works ranging from *Blue Feather* by Paul A. Jones (1953) to *A Thief of Time* by the well-known mystery writer Tony Hillerman (1988). In these works, Kokopelli takes on many guises, from itinerant Zuni to Toltec nobleman, and operates in many venues, engaging himself in plots from the magical and mysterious to the salacious.

The reasons for this Kokopellimania are many. The near-universal appeal of the flute and the magic its music can evoke may be part of the reason. It is probably no accident that the growing popularity of recorded Native American flute music parallels the rise of Kokopelli enthusiasm. The ancient belief, perhaps still subliminally present, that touching a hunchback assures good luck (Webb 1936: 8) may be another reason. An ideological admixture consisting of ecological and environmental concerns along with a liberal dose of New Age philosophy are also undoubtedly involved. New Age thinking, which freely operates with such popularized notions as "Great Spirit," "Mother Earth,"[1] "dream catcher," and so on (notions that have no linguistic counterpart in most Native American cultures), probably also helped pave the way for the acceptance of Kokopelli as a nostalgic icon of the noble savage. Anderson (1976: 39) seems to imply that "Kokopelli's masculine allure" has a particular attraction for women, for he suggests—totally without justification—that "the bulk of Kokopelli research" was "gathered and compiled by women." Neary (1992: 76), speculating about the popularity of "this spooky, jaunty fellow with the humpback, the flute, and the erect phallus" and why "all these people want to take him and his beguiling cousins home with them," answers his query in a fashion consistent with his "Kokopelli Kitsch" article:

> Well, maybe he is magic, maybe he and the other powerful symbols we call petroglyphs do contain some mystical ancient force. Maybe the hands of the artists who carved him and his fellow rock figures were moved by some elemental command that stirs us, too. Touching something deep inside themselves, they thus managed to pull off the old abracadabra that is every artist's dream: to reach across time to touch us, too, with their bold, stark mysterious talismans, poetry in stone that speaks in a language we didn't even know we understood.

Another reason may be the desire on the part of many people to mitigate the effects of modern high-tech society, which some see as impersonal, sterile, and without mystery. The phrase "high tech, high touch" has become popular in describing the attractiveness of a wide range of activities—from baking your own bread and growing your own vegetables to building things without

---

1. The notion of Mother Earth, as "one of the most well-known, firmly established, and emotion-laden figures in Native American religions" (Gill 1987: 1), has clearly been debunked by Gill. After a thorough review of the ethnographic and scholarly literature on native North America, he comes to the conclusion that "'Mother Earth' has come into existence in America largely during the last one hundred years and that her existence stems primarily from two creative groups: scholars and Indians" (Gill 1987: 7).

power tools—anything that harks back to a perceived simpler time. Along the lines of recapturing mystery, Tisdale (1993: 214) believes that interest in Kokopelli reflects the increased interest of the general public in the spiritual and mystical ways of Native Americans. Participating in things Kokopelli may be a way to achieve some "high touch" in one's life and participate in something a bit exotic and mysterious, but in a safe and ultimately effortless way.

In a more ominous vein, Lewis-Williams (1995: 320–21) has made observations regarding South African rock art that may apply to the Kokopelli phenomenon. In his view the wholesale appropriation of rock art motifs on the likes of coffee mugs and T-shirts may reflect a process of recontextualization that begins when Western capitalism meets indigenous culture: those who once held such motifs to be mythic and holy can become an impediment to the spread of Western culture. When the spread has almost reached the point of total assimilation of the indigenous culture and early conflicts have almost been forgotten, the process then becomes masked by a gloss of fun, in this instance opening the way to the depiction of Kokopelli in numerous trivializing ways solely for commercial gain.

The overriding reason, however, for the Kokopelli phenomenon may be the explosive growth of interest in rock art. Long almost entirely neglected in American anthropology and archaeology, academically oriented studies in rock art have made tremendous advances in the last two decades, to the point where rock art is emerging as a new scientific discipline. With the development of rock art as a separate field of study, there has come about an increasing awareness of petroglyphic and pictographic designs among the mainstream public. Confronted with this visually captivating and emotionally stirring paleoimagery, the most frequently asked question quickly became "What does it mean?" Puzzled and frustrated by a plethora of mysterious motifs whose creators had been extinct for many centuries, and in some cases, several millennia, people soon embarked on second-guessing the "meanings" of the individual motifs. In the process of such speculative endeavors, identifiable elements such as that of a "flute man" became revelations. Here, finally, was something to hold on to, something that was recognizable and hence interpretable.

Figure 2: Fluteplayer attributes
*The wide variety of fluteplayer attributes, including figure morphology, pos-
ture, orientation and size, flute configuration, and other associated accoutre-
ments, reflects the multi-functional position the fluteplayer must have
enjoyed, over time, in the prehistoric Native American religious systems.
Many of the fluteplayer attributes, including those of the bird-headed figures
(b, c, f, j), seem to indicate that the image depicted was a religious personage
with considerable magical power. The sample of fluteplaying images shown
here, from widely separated areas in Arizona (b, c, e, i, j, l, m), New Mexico
(d, h, k), and Utah (a, f, g), illustrates a few of the dramatic variations in the
conceptualization of the figure over time and space.*

The fluteplayer rock art image originated in the Four Corners area, probably along the southern edge of Black Mesa, north of the present-day Hopi villages. This inference is based on the presence of very large concentrations of fluteplayer designs (more than 175 at one site), as well as the figure's wide variation in morphology, attributes, elaborations, and associations. While the specific reason for the creation of the fluteplayer is unknown, such images were first created as early as A.D. 800 and in significant numbers by at least 1000. The earliest depictions were generally simple stick or outlined figures with an obvious flute but had no hump and were nonithyphallic (did not have an erect penis). Subsequent to the creation of the basic figure, the fluteplayer symbol spread throughout the Four Corners area. Fluteplayers have been identified as far east as the Rio Grande River Valley area, north to the Great Salt Lake region, west to the western Grand Canyon region, and south to the valleys below the Mogollon Rim. The correlation of this widest distribution with the maximum extent of the pueblo-dwelling Native American farming cultures of prehistoric times is striking and suggests that the fluteplayer image is uniquely characteristic of these cultures.

As a result of the diffusion of the fluteplayer rock art icon and its continued evolution in its region of origin, distinctive regional variations developed. In the southern Black Mesa region in Arizona, elaborate embellishments to the basic fluteplayer figure were common from 1100 to 1400. In some areas, specifically the San Juan Basin of southern Utah and the upper Rio Grande River Valley in New Mexico, the images often exhibited humps and were ithyphallic, sometimes exaggerated to such an extent as to dominate the figure. Where and how these additional attributes originated is not known. Eventually, fluteplayer figures became so varied and elaborate that it is now difficult to reconstruct the original morphological concept of the figure.

After some five hundred years of use, the fluteplayer image began to disappear. First, the image became smaller and less dominant, and then it gradually vanished completely. In most regions fluteplayer rock art images were no longer made after 1400, while in a few areas they were produced as late as 1600. The demise of the fluteplayer image was a natural cultural occurrence taking place prior to substantial contact between its Native American creators and the intrusive Anglo culture.

While an in-depth analysis and presentation of the rock art fluteplayer would merit a book-length treatise of its own, certain archaeological observations are introduced in the captions of the twelve illustrations accompanying this work. They touch on the distribution of the motif over the Colorado Plateau and adjacent regions, single out certain stylistic patterns, and give an idea of the variety of attributes and associations encountered with the image. They also show the motif as a decorative element on prehistoric ceramics. A more realistic impression of the diversity of fluteplayer images can be obtained from the color plates.

About three decades ago, Klaus Wellmann (1970: 1678), one of the great pioneering figures in the study of North American rock art, was still able to claim that only a small circle of *cognoscenti* was familiar with "the euphonious name of 'Kokopelli.'" Today, the misnomer has nearly turned into a household word in the American Southwest. With the joy of recognizing the rock art emblem of a fluteplayer came the relative ease of this pronounceable Indian word. This linkage of facile recognition and pronounceability may have contributed to the widespread acceptance of the term in an otherwise relatively linguaphobic society.

Whatever the reasons may have been for propelling Kokopelli to such a high level of public awareness, in its wake came a rapid increase in Kokopelli-related literature. While much of the early ethnographic writing on this subject was anchored, to a good degree, in bona fide field investigation, the publications following them were increasingly fanciful and derivative. A sampling of sources from the prolific literature on the topic helps illustrate the process of misunderstanding that brought us to the current state of affairs.

We can begin with the spelling of the name of the Hopi kachina from which "Kokopelli" is derived. To be sure, early archaeologists and ethnologists were not scientifically trained phoneticians, nor were reference works such as Hopi dictionaries or grammars available to be consulted. To my knowledge, the first reference to the god's name occurs in Fewkes (1898: 663), where it is transcribed as "Kokopeli." Five years later (1903: 110), however, he uses "Kokopelli." Other spellings encountered in the literature are "Kokopele" (Titiev 1939: 91), "Kokopölö" (Colton 1949: 35), "Kókopilau" (Waters 1963: 38), and "Kókopölö" (Dockstader 1954: 28). Dockstader's usage is closest to the orthographically correct version, "Kookopölö," with the stress on the long vowel in the first syllable.

In oral tales, Kookopölö is occasionally referred to as Kokopöltiyo, literally, "Kookopölö Boy," which explains the form "Kokopeltiyo" cited by Titiev (1939: 92 n. 8). The female counterpart to the male god is Kokopölmana, "Kookopölö Girl." Unlike Kookopölö, however, whose name is stressed on the first syllable because of its long vowel, "Kokopölmana" is accented on the second syllable. In accordance with Hopi stress rules, a polysyllabic word receives its primary stress on the second syllable if the first syllable is short, which is the case in "Kokopölmana."

It is understandable that investigators untrained in phonetics would have difficulty capturing the proper sound qualities of a linguistic term foreign to them. Given this, it is then not advisable to take a linguistically unverified spelling such as "Kokopelli" and employ it as a departure point for cross-cultural speculations. The statement by one fluteplayer researcher that the Hopi "Kokopelli (or Kokopilli)" might be "ideologically and aesthetically" connected with the Aztec "Xochipilli" (Salter 1960: 16) is, at the very least, on shaky ground.

Similar attempts have been made to unlock the etymology of "Kookopölö." Dockstader (1954: 28), in the context of discussing the close cultural ties between Hopi and Zuni societies, suggests that "Koko" (correctly, "Kokko"), Zuni for "kachina," might be useful in establishing the origin of certain Hopi kachinas: "The very use of the Zuni word *Koko* is of help in tracing some of these Hopi beings, for a few bear names suggestive of hybrid origin. Kókopölö, Kókosori, Kokoshshóskoya, and perhaps Qöqöqlö, are examples of Hopi Kachinas now fully accepted, which seem to indicate this incorporation."

As it turns out, probably only the name "Kókosori" (correctly, "Kokosori," with the accent on the second syllable) was borrowed from Zuni. "Kokoshshóskoya" (correctly, "Kokosorhoya") is simply "Kokosori" with the Hopi diminutive suffix -*hoya* (not the misspelled -*koya*). "Qöqöqlö" (correctly, "Qööqöqlö") is the Third Mesa kachina name for the Second Mesa "Qöqlö," an authentic Hopi name that is phonemically quite distant from the Zuni word *kokko*, "mask" and "masked dancer." Edmund Ladd (personal communication, 1995) confirms that there is no evidence that the Hopi "Kookopölö" incorporates the Zuni *kokko*, since no equivalent term is attested in Zuni culture on which the borrowed Hopi name could have been based. Patterson-Rudolph's (1990: 50) categorical statement that "the name 'Kokopelli,' as commonly used for all kinds of fluteplayers, comes from the mythical locust-like insect character who is able to bring rain and fertility for the people of Zuni" is therefore also unfounded.

Waters (1963: 38) discusses the elements *koko* and *-pilau*, assigning the former the meaning "wood" and the latter "hump." While *-pilau* in its proper spelling of *pölö* does translate as "hump," the bisyllabic *koko* actually means "burrowing owl" in Hopi. However, the first part of "Kookopölö," correctly transcribed with its long vowel as *kooko*, does not occur as an isolated morpheme in the Hopi language. Therefore, any acoustic semblance to *koho*, the correct word for "dry stick, wood," must be ruled out.

Young (1990: 14) speculates that the suffix *-pelli* may represent the Hopi name for the desert robber fly. Similar to *pilau* above, *-pelli* is just another misspelling of the Hopi *pölö*, a legitimate word denoting "ball, hump, bump, stub." The etymon of *kooko-*, however, remains obscure and is therefore untranslatable.

The roles, functions, and overall characterizations attributed to Kokopelli in the published literature are legion. While some home in on the true properties of the Hopi god, others explore uncharted regions of speculative interpretation.

To the Hopis, Kookopölö is a kachina god whose foremost aspects are human and vegetal fertility, as will be demonstrated below in the discussion of Kookopölö in Hopi ethnography. In the literature, however, he emerges as a personage with multiple roles, most of which are not borne out by Hopi ethnographic evidence. This misleading portrayal of Kookopölö is caused not only by the confusion of the fluteless kachina with the flute-endowed *maahu*, or cicada (as discussed below in the chapter on the cicada in Hopi ethnography), but is also caused by the fact that many of the god's supposed functions appear to be simply extrapolated from depictions of the fluteplayer motif in rock art and from other prehistoric artistic manifestations.

Parsons, for example, in editing Stephen's *Hopi Journal* (1936: 338 n. 1), was apparently the first to use the appellation "hunchback" in connection with the Hopi Kookopölö. Next, Hawley (1937: 645) introduces the concept of "the hunch-backed fluteplayer." As Brill (1984: 4) rightly points out, Hawley never reveals whether the appellation "was adopted out of a desire to associate Kokopelli with local humpbacked prehistoric anthropomorphs" that she and others had observed "in the vicinity of the historic and prehistoric homelands. Regardless of whether or not Hawley recorded this term or ... invented it ... it appears to have had a 'snowballing' effect culminating in the frequent and almost blind acceptance of the term as a synonym for Kokopelli." Parsons (1939: 381) employs the variant term "hump backed flute player" as she equates the locust (correctly, cicada) with Kookopölö. Colton (1949: 35), finally, trumps the others with the "Hump-backed Flute Player Kachina." Only fourteen years later, Waters (1963: 61) already can confidently refer to the god as "the well-known humpbacked flute player."

Similar to this process of acceptance of Kokopelli as a hunchback is his characterization as a hunter by Lambert (1967: 400). This misassociation of the god with hunting activities can be traced back to Parsons (1926: 206 n. 3), where she claims that he is a "hunting kachina." Referring the reader to a source in Fewkes and Stephen (1892: 211 n. 1), she misconstrues their statement that "the Ko-kü-li is a hunting Ká-tcí-na." "Ko-kü-li" is a corrupt form of "Qööqöqlö," who is indeed a hunting kachina. Kookopölö is not a hunting kachina, however, and she apparently confused the two. This hunting association surfaces again in Wellmann (1970: 1678) when he refers to Kokopelli as a "hunting magician."

Kokopelli's supposed dwarfism is widely discussed (sometimes with medical evidence) (Lambert 1957: 106; Cawley 1966: 285; Vogl 1970: 599; Wellmann 1970: 1679; Wright 1993: 17; Payne 1976: 34). He also is seen as a prehistoric Kilroy, Casanova, minstrel, god, lecher, or insect (Young 1965: 39, 41); rain maker (Lambert 1967: 400); rain priest and Don Juan (Wellmann 1970: 1678); creator, culture hero, transformer, forerunner of the savior, and regional variant of the universal trickster archetype (Wellmann 1974: 2); fighter, not a lover (Davis 1975: 7); powerful medicine man, shaman, healer, and seducer of young girls (Ritter and Ritter 1977: 68); similar to the fauns and satyrs of Greco-Roman antiquity (Aron 1981: 13); and as a symbol of peace and brotherhood among the various Indian tribes (Herrera in Seymour 1988: 174).

He is also characterized as a *puchteca,* a traveling Aztec or Toltec trader from central Mexico (Wright 1993: 17); Water Sprinkler (Young 1990: iii); Pan or Orpheus-like mediator between heaven and earth, the connecting link between worlds and master of ceremonies (Acatos in Bruggman and Acatos 1990: 212); bringer of corn and seducer of women (Conway 1993: 117, 125); spirit of the Great Plains (Anati 1993: 143); perky, mischievous little fellow (Lyon 1995: 11); hero with a thousand faces and shapeshifter (Hill 1995: 7, 17); and as a cross between a magician, the Pied Piper, and Johnny Appleseed, an exemplar of the Hopis' ability to achieve harmony with negative parts of their environment, in this case the locust (cicada), a grasshopper-like pest insect of the family Acrididae that sometimes ravages crops (Caduto and Bruchac 1988: 151–52). Finally, in the best modern pop-psychology terms, he can be seen as a "dancing, flute-playing, circular celebrant" who fulfills "our root need to integrate and harmonize the fragments of our existence" (Hill 1995: 16).

How are all the foregoing flights of fancy possible? One possible reason is that Hopi ethnographic field research concerning the fluteplayer has been at a virtual standstill for several decades. Mallery (1893: 511–12), who seems to have been the first to investigate rock art depictions of the fluteplayer, still sought information from "the most intelligent of the old Moki priests."[2] As a result, he uses the term "flageolet priest" in reference to what appears to be a fluteplayer image. The last time a genuine tidbit of cultural significance was collected in regard to the motif occurred over thirty years ago in the course of Turner's rock art survey in the Glen Canyon area prior to the construction of Glen Canyon Dam. Hopi consultants who accompanied Turner during this survey, when confronted with the motif at a number of rock art panels, repeatedly insisted that the fluteplayer, whether humped or not, was not "Kokopele" (Turner 1963: 22, 50 fig. 13, and 70 fig. 94). Nor did Thybony (in Hirschmann and Thybony 1994: 41) find that Hopis reacted favorably to this equation when he made the mistake of calling the depiction of a fluteplayer on a ring a

---

2. The name "Moki," commonly used to refer to Southwestern Pueblo Indians in pre-twentieth-century writings, seems to be derived from "Muukwi" (Edmund Ladd, personal communication), the Zuni name for "Hopi." Mispronounced by the Spanish conquistadores as "Moki," the appellation became offensive to the Hopis because of the word's proximity to the Hopi verb *mooki,* "to die."

Kokopelli. Instead, he was corrected that the figure represented a Lahlanhoya. Correctly spelled *leelenhoya* in First Mesa and *lelenhoya* in Third Mesa dialects, the term, which actually means "flutist" and, in a modern sense, "musician," is apparently a Hopi attempt to capture the Anglo notion of "fluteplayer." While fluteplayers in the rock art are typically termed *maahu*, "the cicada," by Hopi consultants, and not *lelenhoya*, the response that Thybony received unequivocally refutes their designation as "Kokopelli." Most recently Secakuku (1995: 18), the first Hopi to officially comment on this misnomer in a publication of his own, unequivocally states that "Kokopölö is a katsina with a humpback. He is not a Flute player, though he has been mistakenly referred to as such."

Fluteplayer research has seldom been grounded in the Hopi language itself. Learning a foreign language can be a formidable task, difficult enough if this language is a member of the Indo-European language family, and even more so for one such as Hopi that is outside this linguistic affiliation. Library research that draws only on recorded English sources is the easier course by far and is the course taken by many.

This approach has been the fate of research on the fluteplayer motif ever since Waters (1963: 38) equated the humpbacked fluteplayer with "the kachina named Kókopilau." Despite this and similar statements, even a casual collector of Hopi kachina dolls should have been baffled by the fact that the *tihu*, "carved figurine," of the deity is never equipped with a flute, except by young carvers who have bowed to Anglo market demands. Similarly, an observer of the public kachina parade at the occasion of the Hopi Powamuy ceremony,[3] or a spectator at a Hopi kachina night dance, should certainly find it odd that the kachina never carries a flute.

While the earlier ethnographic accounts of Stephen, Fewkes, Voth, Curtis, Beaglehole, Parsons, and Titiev—to mention some of the better-known recorders of early Hopi life and culture—were based on solid and substantial field-

---

3. In accordance with Hopi preference, all terms for Hopi ceremonies will be cited in Hopi, employing the pertinent combining forms in conjunction with such words as ceremony, ritual, dance, and so forth. Thus, instead of "Bean dance," the phrase "Powamuy ceremony" will be used, and instead of "Flute ceremony," "Len ceremony." Clan names, on the other hand, are represented in English, according to Hopi preference.

work, their findings undoutedly would have been more insightful and reliable had they been conducted in the Hopi vernacular and published in Hopi as well as in English. Unfortunately, the linguistic tools to accomplish this were not available to many of the early researchers, although individual Hopi terms for concepts and artifacts occur throughout their works. Since then, the study of Hopi culture through the medium of the Hopi language itself has largely been neglected. While this approach does not require complete fluency in the language, an in-depth comprehension of the phonological, morphological, syntactic, and semantic properties of the Hopi language is required.

There are two reasons why Hopi ethnography is so well suited to shedding light on the fluteplayer mystery. First, the misnomer "Kokopelli" that is commonly applied to the motif by non-Hopis derives, as we have seen, from "Kookopölö," a Hopi kachina god associated with the assassin or robber fly, an insect of the family Asilidae. Second, although there is no evidence that the fluteplayer motif originated in prehistoric Hopi culture, no other modern Puebloan culture in the Southwest supplies as many ethnographic clues to its identification. From all indications the model underlying the motif is an insect from the superfamily Homoptera—the cicada, known to the Hopis as *maahu*.

The chapters in part 1 clarify the Hopi ethnographic record in regard to the humpbacked Hopi deity Kookopölö and the cicada. To the greatest extent possible, this clarification is carried out from the perspective of relevant Hopi ethnographic data. Of these, folk statements that I collected over the years directly from Hopi consultants in their own vernacular will be considered primary. Where applicable, they will be supplemented by reliable secondary materials found in the literature. The ethnographic data are rounded out in part 2 by six Hopi folktales that feature Kookopölö or the cicada in the role of protagonist or supporting character.

To guarantee the highest degree of cultural authenticity, all primary folk statements are presented bilingually, with Hopi as the donor language preceding all corresponding English translations. While I am aware that indigenous ethnography itself is not always perfect and may even be erroneous, at least it is so from the cultural insider's point of view. I am also aware of a certain amount of repetitiveness that is inherent in some of the folk statements. This is however unavoidable when statements are collected from many individuals.

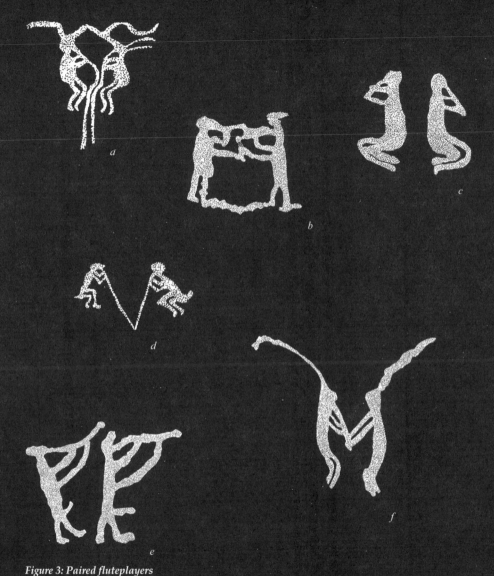

Figure 3: Paired fluteplayers
Most fluteplayers occur as single images, but grouped or clustered depictions, up to ten in number (see Figures 6g and 10g, i), are attested. The most frequent groupings appear to be clusters of two or three figures (f) (see Figures 6a, c, f, j, 9i, k, 10j). However, twinned (f) and symmetrically paired images (a, b, c, d, e) are relatively uncommon.

Part 1

ELEMENTS OF KOKOPELLI IN HOPI ETHNOGRAPHY

Kookopölö, the Robber Fly Kachina

The Insect Model for Kookopölö

The natural model for the kachina Kookopölö is an insect. Fewkes (1898: 663 n. 4) was the first to point out this entomological connection. According to him, he learned of it during excavation work at the prehistoric Hopi ruin of Sikyatki when one of the Indian laborers called his "attention to a large Dipteran insect which he called 'Kokopeli' [correctly, *kookopölö*]." A few years later, in his collection "Hopi Katcinas Drawn by Native Artists" (1903: 86), Fewkes reiterates this observation without, however, identifying the insect in question. Referring to a remark attributed by Parsons to Titiev (Stephen 1936: 1142) that the insect is humpbacked and "does not desist from copulating when disturbed," Parsons (1938: 337 n. 2) wonders whether the dragonfly, "a sacrosanct Pueblo insect," might be the candidate for the model of Kookopölö. "Dragonfly is a persistent copulator," as she points out, adding, however, that taxonomically it is "a neuropterous insect." Insects of the order Neuroptera typically have four net-veined wings, whereas those in the order Diptera have only a single pair of membranous wings. By the time Colton published the first edition of his *Hopi Kachina Dolls with a Key to Their Identification* (1949: 35), he had succeeded in correctly identifying the insect, for he refers to Kookopölö as the "Assassin or Robber Fly Kachina."

The family of robber flies, scientifically known as Asilidae, belongs to a number of "blood-sucking families" (Linsenmaier 1972: 257). Being highly aggressive predators, they "catch insect prey on the wing" (O'Toole 1985: 28), diving like hawks "onto the back of their prey" (Linsenmaier 1972: 257). Equipped with a poisonous beak "whose paralytic action is designed for the soft neck region of an insect" (Linsenmaier 1972: 259), they possess a very pronounced hump that Capinera (1995: 86) sees as a diagnostic feature of Kookopölö.

The mini-tale in Text 1 illustrates the term *kookopölö* in the sense of "robber fly." Frequently, however, the full form is contracted to *kopö*, as may be gathered from the subsequent Hopi folk citations.

Text 1

Aliksa'i. Yaw Orayve yeesiwngwu-
niqw ayam yaw Pitsinvastsomove
Kookopölö ki'yta. Noq pang kya pi
pay hisat naapvöningwuniqw yaw
hakiy angqe'niqw yaw pam pangqw
hakiy aw kuyvangwu, tataqölöt
angqw. Pu' hakiy aw pangqawngwu,
"Pitsintsuku, pitsintsuku." Pu' yaw
pam ahoy aqwhaqami supkima-
ngwu. Pay yukhaqam paasavo.

Aliksa'i. People were living at Oraibi.
Over there at Pitsinvastsomo [Cotton
Field Hill], a robber fly had made his
home. Through that area, long ago,
there used to lead a trail, and each
time someone went along on it, this
robber fly looked out from a large
hole in the rock and cried, "Cotton
tip, cotton tip!" And then he disappeared back into his hole again. This
is as far as the story goes.

Text 2 describes the appearance and some of the robber fly's characteristics from the Hopi point of view.

Text 2

Kopö pam piw himu pay masa'ytaqa
puuyawnumngwu, pay momot aa-
sayhaqam. Pay piw motsovu'y-
kyangw angqw qöötsa tuuwuhiwtangwu. Noq pam i' pi masa'ytaqa
pam pay wuuyoqat poosi'ytangwuqat pangqaqwangwu. Kopö pööla'y-
taqa pi antsa pi puuyawnumngwu.

The robber fly is a winged creature
about the size of a bee. It has a snout
from which runs a white stripe. People also say that the robber fly has
large eyes and is truly hunchbacked
as it flies about.

Apparently, the noise created by the insect is a distinctive feature that
caught the attention of the Hopi.

Text 3

Kopö pi pay mi'ningwu, pay ura himu masa'ytaqa, hiisayhoya. I' kopö
puuyalte' pay tu'mumtingwu. Pay

The robber fly is a small insect with
wings. When it flies, it produces a
hum that sounds like *vvvöm*. That's

vvvöm kitangwu. Pay panhaqam pam tuwat hinta. Pam pay maahut qa an leelenngwu.

how a robber fly is. It does not flute like a cicada, though.

The folk statement in Text 4 clearly equates the insect with the kachina Kookopölö.

Text 4

Pam kopö hin piw töqtingwu pay hakiy angqe puuyalte'. Katsinat taawi'at piw kopöt töötökiyat aw sootapnangwu. Pay sootapne' pepeq me pay hingqawngwu, "Vövövö."

The robber fly makes a strange noise as it flies around a person. The song of Kookopölö, the kachina, ends just like the sounds the insect makes. For when the kachina song ends, it says, "Vövövö."

According to Hopi belief, the noise produced by the robber fly is reminiscent of Hopi speech. It can therefore be understood and is said to comment on whatever activity a person happens to be engaged in. Texts 5 and 6 illustrate this point.

Text 5

Kopö pi yaw hakiy piw su'an hiita aa'awnangwu.

They say the robber fly is the one that tells you what is right.

Text 6

I' pay kopö wuko'umumutaqat töqmangwu. I' pay puuyawnumngwu, pay hiisayhoya. Wuuyoq tootovit epniiqeniqw i' hakiy suupan aw hingqawngwu.

Pay nu' hisat tumat kwasintaqe nu' sunala. Qa haqam hakniqw nu' naala pepeq qööhi'ykyangw pay hiita

The robber fly makes a deep humming sound. It flies around and is quite small. Bigger than a large fly, it seems to be talking to you.

Once I was all alone firing a piki stone. There was nobody around, and I had a fire going all by myself, sitting in the shade of a peach tree.

sipaltsokit kiisiwniyat atpipaq qa-
tuqw i' kopö angqaqw puuyawnuma.
Inutsva puuyalti. Nit suupan hingqawu, "Qa kwasi," suupan kita inumi.
Pu' pay angqe puuyawnumkyangw
pu' pay piw inumi pu', "Qa kwasi,"
suupan inumi kita.
      "Son pi qa kwasini. Nu' aw
wukoqöhi'yta," nu' aw kita.
      Pay pam hakiy aw yaw hing-
qawngwuqat pangqaqwa. Hiita hak
hintsakqw put pangqawngwu. Noq
hiita hak hintsakqw put aw hayaw-
taqat hakiy yaw aw hingqawu. Pay
hapi hakiy lee'elanta.
      Nu' pu' tumat kwasintaqw oovi
inumi pangqawu, "Qa kwasi."

Suddenly, a robber fly came flying
along. As it flew over my head, it
seemed to be saying, "It's not done."
Flying around it insisted once more,
"It's not done."
      "It's bound to get done," I re-
plied. "I have a big fire going under
it."
      People say that the robber fly is
talking to you. It comments on whatever you are doing. Or rather it says
something that sounds similar to
what you are doing.
      To me, firing a piki stone, it said,
"It's not fired."

Interestingly enough, the expression *qa kwasi*, "it is not done," which in this context refers to the firing of a *piki* stone, is equally applicable to the cooking of food. More significantly, however, it can also translate as "it is not a penis." I am convinced that this ambiguity in Text 6 is no coincidence and that the play on words is an intentional sexual innuendo, considering the insect's overt mating behavior, as is evident from Text 7.

Text 7

Pu' ephaqam lööyöm kopöt naami
pite' puma piw naatsoptangwu.
Naami huurtingwu, oovi qa iits
naamatapngwu.

Occasionally, when two robber flies
meet, they really copulate. As a rule,
they get so stuck together that they
do not let go of each other right
away.

This apparent mating compulsion that Hopis perceive in the insect may be exaggerated from an entomological perspective. Nevertheless, it expresses their view of things and may actually have been conditioned by the sexually explicit behavior that is displayed by the two kachina deities modeled on the insect, Kookopölö and Kokopölmana. Also of interest in this connection is the observation in Text 8 that the robber fly, as a symbol of life force, was once prayed to by Hopi women to undo barrenness.

Text 8

Pam yaw pi pay qatsit piw tu'awi'ytangwu. Pay puma lööyömnen pay kya pi puma naami hintsakngwu, pay naatsoptaqat antsakngwu. Niikyangw put taaqat suru'at wuutit aw wiwtangwu. Pan kur tuwat puma natsoptuwi'ytangwu.

Puma qatsit tu'awi'ytaqw Hopiit pumuy angqw ngahulalwangwu. Pay himuwa wuuti qa tilawe' pu' paasat pam pumuy amumi okiw tuwat naawaknangwu, kopötuy amumi. Puma pumuy amumi tuuvinglalwangwu, wuuti himuwa okiw paapu tiitaniqey oovi puma momoyam pumuy amumi put tuuvinglalwangwu. Pay pi ima haqawat Hopimomoyam qa tilalwaqw pay okiw himuwa naawaknangwu pumuy amumi. Pay hoomat akw pay okiw amumi okiwlalwangwu. Pay pi amumi naanawakne' pu' pay amumi pangqaqwangwu, "Okiw nu' qa tilawqe oovi nu' as tinawaknakyangw nu' qa tihut qa aniwnangwuniiqe oovi nu' okiw umumi naawakna."

They say the robber fly symbolizes life. Whenever there are two of them, they usually have sex, just like a human couple. As a rule, the male's tail is hooked to the female. This is their way of copulating.

Since the two robber fly insects symbolize life, the Hopis get beneficial powers from them. When a woman is barren, she will pray to the two insects. The women ask them that they may be able to give birth, for some Hopi women cannot have children. As a rule they use sacred cornmeal when they pray, speaking like this, "Poor me, I'm not bearing any offspring. I want a child, but because I'm not producing one, I'm asking you."

Why Hopis make so much of the robber fly's copulation habits is not readily obvious to the entomologist. As Peter Price (1995 personal communication) assures me, while the robber fly is commonly seen copulating, this is not an extraordinary trait as far as insects are concerned. However, among insects in Arizona, robber flies are very conspicuous and can easily be observed both hunting and mating, since they take up fixed stations on rocks and other places. Also, while the copulating behavior of the robber fly may not be extreme, once the sexually overt behavior of the kachina was culturally established, this notion may have reinforced the perception that the insect too was an ardent copulator.

Kookopölö's Appearance and Paraphernalia

Text 9 contains a Hopi description of the kachina deity Kookopölö.

Text 9

Pam Kookopölö pi pay kwaatsit aw pakiwtangwu. Oomiq motsovu'ytangwu. Pam silaqvut angqw yukiwtangwu. Kookopölö paykomuy tsuku'ytaqat motsovu'ytangwu. Put pay hoomat silaqvut ang mokyaatat pantaqat pam motsovu'ytangwu. Pam qömvit taywa'ytangwu. Pu' paasat pam yangqe qötövaqe qöötsat tuuwuhiwtangwu. Öyingaqw pas aakwayngyavoq tsönmiq pitsiwtangwu. Pu' ngölöwtaqat poosi'ytangwu. Ura mi' Kwasa'ykatsina pan poosi'ytangwu. Oovi ngölö'vo.

Pam qa yaqa'ytangwu. Pay panis oovi piw paalangput naqvu'ytangwu. Pay suukw piw nakwa'ytangwu, mita, kwaahut suruyat. Pu' pi

Kookopölö always wears a mask. From it points up a snout that is fashioned from corn husk. Actually, Kookopölö has a three-pointed snout. The individual prongs of the snout are made out of corn husk and contain sacred cornmeal. His face is black. All the way across his head, from his chin to his neck, runs a white stripe. His eyes have a corner that bends up and around just like those of the Kwasa'ykatsina.

He has no nose. His ears are typically red. He also has a feather tied to his head that is an eagle tail feather. Now that the white man has come to live here, the kachina wears an undershirt and underpants. As

pay Paahaanam yesqw oovi pu' pay
Kookopölö aatöqenapnat angqw pakiwtangwu. Pu' piw aatöqehovinap-
na'ytangwu. Pu' hopitotsi'ykyangw
honhokyasmi'ytangwu.

Put motsovu'at mit tu'awi'ytangwu, pay i' tutskwava himu pay
lomahintaniqat oovi pam put tu'a-
wi'ytangwu. Pu' uuyit piw pam
enang tu'awi'ytangwuniiqe oovi put
angqw hooma. Putakw pam enang
naawaknangwuniqw oovi.

footwear he has the reddish brown
buckskin moccasins with colored
ankle bands.

Kookopölö's snout signifies that
the plants that grow on the land will
be nice and green. It also symbolizes
maize. That's the reason for the sacred cornmeal inside the prongs. For
with it the kachina prays.

Not mentioned in the Hopi text is the black and white ruff that is worn
around the neck. According to Lomatuway'ma (Seymour 1988: 271), it is made
of cotton rags and "curved as the kachinas humped back, which makes him
stand in a stooped position." Nor is there any reference to "a white circle with
diametrical lines drawn in black" on each side of the head as Fewkes (1903:
110) reports. The rosette that he refers to may actually occur only on the mask
of the First Mesa Kookopölö.

Curiously enough, none of the illustrations or carved *tihu* in the literature
portray the god with a three-pronged snout. Of all the kachinas illustrated in
Wright's *Kachinas: A Hopi Artist's Documentary*, only the Kwasa'ytaqa (1973:
39) and the Korowiste (1973: 101), the latter being the Zuni model for the former, sport such a snout. Since my consultant likens Kookopölö's eyes to those
of the Kwasa'ytaqa or Kwasa'ykatsina (Text 9), it is likely that the comparison
by oversight also carried over to Kookopölö's snout.

Kookopölö's mouth protrusion, typically referred to in Hopi as *motsovu*,
"snout," has been the source of much speculation ever since Hawley (1937:
645) intimated that the end-blown flute, so obvious in the postulated prehistoric analog of "Kokopelli, the hunch-backed flute player," might have disappeared over time and been replaced by a snout. Such explanatory acrobatics
are not needed once the cultural equation between fluteplayer and Kookopölö

is revealed as a case of mistaken identity. *Leena,* "the flute," still has a major place in the ceremonial life of present-day Hopi. Foremost, it is the distinguishing instrument of the two Len societies, whose ceremonies are based on it. Leenangwkatsina, "Flute kachina," who appears as part of a group of Soyohömkatsinam, "Mixed kachinas," dances with a flute; unlike the Sakwalen and Masilen society members, however, he does not play it. According to Colton (1970: 43), a flute was also carried by the Nuvaktsina, "Snow kachina," and by the Hospowikatsina, "Roadrunner kachina" (Colton 1970: 67). None of my consultants was able to confirm this claim. Finally, Palhikwtiyo, "Moisture Drinking Boy," carries a flute when he appears as a masked kachina during the night dance of the Saasa'lakt or as an unmasked social dancer during a plaza exhibition of the Paavalhikwt. While in his former role Palhikwtiyo can still be witnessed occasionally, the social Palhikw dance,[1] once performed in the fall of the Hopi ceremonial year, has become extinct. Since the flute survived in conjunction with these Hopi ceremonial personages well into the twentieth century, it does not make sense to suggest that, in the case of Kookopölö, this prominent wind instrument was transformed into a mere snout. Indeed, this never happened, for as I have shown above, it is *maahu,* "the cicada," that is endowed with a flute, and not Kookopölö.

Nor can a single reference to Kookopölö be located in any of the early accounts of Hopi Len ceremonies. Colton's observation (1970: 35), vaguely reiterated by Wright (1973: 109), that Kookopölö will borrow a flute from Leenangwkatsina at the occasion of a Mixed kachina dance, seems to constitute but a spontaneous, nonroutine event. It certainly is not borne out ethnographically. Nor would such a spontaneous gesture suffice to establish a full-blown connection between Kookopölö and the motif of the fluteplayer. Kabotie's (1977: 90) painting of a formation of Kookopölö dancers during a kiva night dance warrants mentioning in this context. In a lengthy comment on the artwork, the artist plainly states that the hunchbacked fluteplayers decorating the kiva wall behind the kachina dancers would not be painted there at all, "but I put them in the painting to show the history behind the Kookopölö" (Seymour

---

1. For photos of a Palhikw dance group, see the Smithsonian Institution (1979: 85) catalogue of the Mora exhibition.

1988: 271). I take such a remark as a clear indication that the conjunction of the Kookopölö kachina and the humpbacked fluteplayer motif, so entrenched in white society, is repeated here as acculturated, not traditional, knowledge. The artist Kabotie was versed in art history and anthropology, and I believe that the linkage between the two entities simply had filtered back to him and in this way became part of the painting.

Kookopölö's most distinguished physical trait is the protrusion on his back, generally referred to as a hump. This trait is borne out by the Hopi term *pölö*, "ball, hump," that is integral to the god's name. Explanatory hypotheses for the hump include physical objects such as burden baskets (Brill 1984: 32), backpacks "inspired by itinerant, long-distance traders" (Hurst and Pachak 1989: 14), or actual pathological deformities. Wellmann (1970: 1679) claims that Webb (1936: 7), in his speculations about the medical implications of hunch-backed figures, "left little doubt that ... tuberculosis of the spine, and it alone, was responsible for the very existence of Kokopelli, the hunchbacked flute-player." Webb, who never mentions the name "Kookopölö," indirectly seems to imply that the kachina's dorsal hump was caused by Pott's disease, a tuber-cular affliction of the spine, for in his illustrations (1936: 17) he uses rock art images of flute-playing "hunchbacks" that were recorded by Kidder and Guernsey (1919: 195). Wellmann (1970: 1679) then goes on to dismiss "Webb's" medical theory, arguing (1974: 2) for a cultural, not a medical, determination of the hump. Cawley (1974: 3) proposes that Kookopölö's hump "was very likely a dorsal kyphosis caused by a juvenile epiphysitis" due to hard work in a flexed position during the formative years. Alpert (1991: 56), however, re-turns to a medical explanation. Convinced that Kookopölö was a living indi-vidual in prehistory who suffered from the effects of tuberculosis of the spine with resulting priapism, she flatly states (1991: 53) that "Kookopölö ... has the characteristic kyphosis (exaggerated posterior convexity), and spinal and joint deformities" of Pott's disease.

Prototypes for the hump have also been sought in non-Hopi cultures. Par-sons (1938: 337), for example, indicates that at the Tewa-speaking First Mesa village of Hano "Kookopölö is equated with Nepokwa'i', 'a big black man' (Kookopölö's mask and body are painted black) who in the tales appears with a buckskin on his back from which to make moccasins for a bride"[2] (Parsons 1926: 206). Grant (1967: 61), in elaborating this suggestion, theorizes that "Nepokwa'i [sic] may be based on Esteban, the Negro of Fray Marcos de Niza's ill-fated 1539 expedition to find the famed Seven Cities of Cibola. Esteban was stoned to death by the Zunis for molesting their women." Cutler (1944: 27) ventures as far as the Andes in Peru to pinpoint the starting point of Kokopelli's ancestry. To him "it seems likely that the ancient Southwestern hunchback was actually a Callahuayo medicine man bringing to North America the character of tunicate maize." Miller (1975: 375) sees a model for the hump outside the Southwest, in Mesoamerica. According to him, the ancestor of Kookopölö might have been Ek Chuah, a pre-Hispanic Maya deity. Equipped with a backpack and a straight staff, he is said to have been the "patron of bee keepers," an association that in Miller's view makes him similar to Kokopelli, who is "associated with insects."

As becomes readily apparent in perusing the literature, most of the speculative hypotheses concerning the origin of Kookopölö's (and Kokopelli's) hump are derived from petroglyphic and pictographic depictions of the fluteplayer. They are not the result of ethnological field work in the course of which Hopi consultants were questioned. To cite one final example of such rock-art-derived speculation, Bartman (1979: 9) postulates that the hump "represents a sort of male pregnancy." The author extrapolates this nonsensical conclusion from a tiny fluteplayer image supplied by Renaud (1938: plate 1, N.M. 53), that in her view not only features a hump but also a "distended stomach."

Apparently, the only ethnographic statement concerning Kookopölö's hump that was obtained from a Hopi is cited by Lambert (1957: 104). According to her, Byron Harvey III, upon showing a photograph of an anthropomorphic stone idol with a humpback to a Hopi, received the following "phallic [sic] interpretation": "The hump of Kokopelli represents babies. He is full of them, so that every time he has relations he makes a baby." None of my consultants was able to confirm this explanation, at least not in regard to Kooko-

---

2. The only specific reference to this personage is found in the Tewa tale titled "The Handmark Boy" (Parsons 1926: 206).

pölö's hump. All my ethnographic materials (see Texts 21–23 below) concur in Kookopölö's sexual potency to father children. This potency, however, is not located in the god's hump but in his loins. Titiev's (1939: 96) citation of a remark by Eggan indirectly seems to verify this point. Apparently Eggan, at the occasion of a Kookopölö night dance, was cautioned by a Hopi "to be friends with Kokopele as they were the ones who sent babies." "Sending babies" is probably an English expression for "making or engendering babies." In the same vein, the reference to the hump as "representing babies" is probably only a metaphorical expression for the god's procreative powers.

Text 10, representing a Kookopölö song, refers in rather nonspecific fashion to the contents of the kachina's hump as consisting of "helpful things."

Text 10

Kookopölölö, Kookopölölö,
Hita'nangwvöla'yta,
hita'nangwvöla'yta.
Kookopölölö, Kookopölölö,
Hita'nangwvöla'yta,
hita'nangwvöla'yta.
Ikuywikiy nu' pööla'yta.
Kookopölölö Paavönmanatuy
Kiisiwvitu, kiisiwvitu,
Vö, vö, vö.

Kookopölölö, Kookopölölö,
Has a hump with helpful things,
has a hump with helpful things.
Kookopölölö, Kookopölölö,
Has a hump with helpful things,
has a hump with helpful things.
I have my water jug in my hump.
Kookopölölö came with shade
for Paavön girls, came with shade.
Vö, vö, vö.

Kookopölölö, Kookopölölö,
Wuutaqa, wuutaqa.
Kookopölölö, Kookopölölö,
Wuutaqa, wuutaqa.
Um nuy kuysivut kuysiptoyanani.
Kookopölölö, wuutaqa.
Aayayvövö, aayayvövö.
Vöve, vövövöve.

Kookopölölö, Kookopölölö,
Old man, old man.
Kookopölölö, Kookopölölö,
Old man, old man.
Give me a water jug,
Kookopölölö, old man.
Aayayvövö, aayayvövö.
Vöve, vövövöve.

Figure 4: Animal fluteplayers
Fluteplaying animal images are extremely rare and appear to be geo-
graphically restricted to a few areas, primarily the upper Rio Grande River Valley.
Rare occurrences have been reported from along the San Juan River (b), an area
south of Black Mesa (e), and the Petrified Forest region (see Figure 2l). Insect-like
fluteplayers are the most numerous (a, e, h), but the identity of the insect depicted
is generally indeterminate.

More specifically, the contents of the hump are revealed in the context of two statements portraying Kookopölö in the role of a Piptuqa, "masked burlesque" or "kachina skit actor." Contrary to Wright's contention (1994: 100), Piptuqas are not clowns but genuine kachinas, for they are prayed to for rain just like other kachinas (Malotki 1991: 54).

Text 11

Hotvelpeq nu' put suus aw taatayi Kookopölö piptuqw. Noq ima tsutskut put pöölayat antsa pan tsawiknaya. Noq pam angqw tangawta, poshuminiqw pu' tuupevu. Pu' mansaala piw enangniqw put pam pay tuuhuyta.

Once in Hotevilla I saw a Kookopölö act as a Piptuqa. When the clowns undid his hump, there were seeds and baked sweet corn inside. Apples, too, which the kachina handed out to the spectators.

Text 12

Pu' piw ephaqam pu' pam imuy tsutskutuy aw piw pitungwu, Kookopölö. Niikyangw pam pööla'ytangwuniqw hisat piptuqw ep nu' piw tsukulawqw ep pam piptu, Kookopölö. Ep pu' nu' put ngu'a, Kookopölöt, niinaniqe. Noq pu' inumi pangqawu, "Haaki, um yep ivölay aqw hintsanni. Nu' pangqw hiita amungem tanga'ynuma."

Inumi kitaqw pu' nu' hölöknaqw ep himu mookiwtaqw pu' nu' oovi put angqw langaknaqw ep hiihimu sipala, melooni, tu'tsi, tuupevu kur mookiwta. Kur pam put pööla'ytaqw yan itam nanapta. Kur pam pep nuutungem nitkyat iikwiwtangwuniiqe

Once in a while a Kookopölö comes to the clowns. Once when I was also clowning, he appeared as a Piptuqa with a hump. I grabbed him to kill him. However, he said to me, "Hold it! Do something to my hump. It's full of things I'm carrying around for you."

No sooner had he told me than I lifted up his shirt. Sure enough, there were things bagged there. As I pulled some out, peaches, melons, roasted corn, and baked sweet corn came to the fore. This is how we realized that these things made up his hump. Kookopölö carries journey food on his back for people, which accounts for oovi pööla'ytangwu pam Kookopölö. Yan itam piw put aw nanapta. Niiqe oovi itam as put niinayaniqw itamumi kita yaw pam hiita itamungem hinvaqw. Noq itam antsa put hölöknayaqe put tutwa hiihiita nunukngwat. Pu' itam put noonova. Pay pi tsuku naap hin hiita nösngwuniqw pu' oovi itam put naanap hin nöönösa. Pan put itam qa niinayaqw oovi pam qa mooki.

his hump. We were just about to kill him when he revealed to us what he had brought for us. As we lifted up his shirt, we discovered all sorts of goodies there. Those we devoured, for a clown eats things any old way, and that's exactly what we did. In this way we did not dispatch him, and he did not die.

Parsons (in Stephen 1936: 1142) had claimed that the contents of Kookopölö's hump consisted of "blankets, belts, and a quart of seeds of which he gave a few to each girl." My own ethnographic information, presented in Text 13, explains that the blankets are "hump stuffers," so to speak. Contrary to Parson's observation, however, the seeds are not handed out to the girls among the spectators but solely to the men. By bestowing seeds on the men, who as farmers are responsible for life-sustaining crops, Kookopölö is clearly portrayed as an instigator of vegetal fertility.

Text 13

Pam pi piw pööla'ytangwu Kookopölöniiqe pay pi pangqw yaw piw na'mangwuy pam pööla'ytangwuqat kitota. Noq pay pi puma Kookopölt hisat ökiiqe pay hiita pay tsatsakwmötsapu'ewakw, pösalhoya'ewakw puma pööla'yyungngwu.

Pam it hiita poshumit, morivosit, kawaysivosit pam pööla'ytangwu. Pu' pay hiita piw enang tuupevu'ewakw pu' pay puuvut pam pep pööla'ytangwu, mi' Kookopölö. Pam

Kookopölö has a hump. According to what people say he has gifts in it. When a group of Kookopölös come, they usually have their humps stuffed with something like cloth or a blanket.

As a rule, Kookopölö has seeds in his hump, such as bean and melon seeds. In addition, baked sweet corn and foods of this nature may be packed in it. The seeds he has as gifts so that all the crops can grow. These

poshumit na'mangwu'yta, soosoy
himu natwani aniwtiniqat oovi. Pam
pay pumuy oovi taataqtuy put
huylawu piiwu. Pay tiitsonaye' pu'
paasat pay hiita tuuhuylalwangwu pi
katsinamniqw pay pumuy amunti-
ngwu. Pam pay tuwat put poshumiy
akw paasat pu' taataqtuy kwatslaw-
ngwu. Pu' pay piw tuupevut enang-
nen pay put piw enang tuuhuylaw-
ngwu.

seeds he distributes among the men.
As soon as the dancing has stopped
and the kachinas hand out presents
to the spectators, he does likewise.
He, however, gives away seeds to the
men. If he also has some sweet corn,
he distributes that too.

The passage in Text 14 leaves no doubt that Kookopölö's hump contains
food and crops. In this role as provider of vital sustenance and vegetal fecundity Kookopölö is actively prayed to by the Hopis.

Text 14

Antsa pam pööla'ytangwu Kookopö-
löniqw pam antsa kur pep it Hopit
piw naat nöösiwqat, natwanit pam
tu'awi'ytaqe pam pep put Hopit
engem piw naat mooki'ytangwu,
pöölayat epe. Paniqw oovi put hakim
piw aw naanawaknangwu, hiita
hakim aniwnayaniqey.
    Pu' pam piw taala' uuyit ang
sonqe waynumngwu, Kookopölö.
Noq paniqw oovi hakim aw naanawakne', "Ta'ay, pay nam itam okiw
hiihiita su'an natwantotaqw a'ni
himu aniwtini." Yan hakim aw lavay-
totingwu. Yan aw naanawaknangwu.
Pu' hakiy antsa hu'wane' pu' haqami

Kookopölö truly has a hump. It symbolizes the Hopi's food and crops.
That's what is wrapped up in it. For
this reason those who want to grow
things pray to the god.
    In summer, then, Kookopölö is
bound to walk among the plants.
That's why they say when they pray
to him, "All right, let's humbly grow
all sorts of things so that there will be
lots of crops." As Kookopölö agrees
and returns to his own home, he will
relate this wish to his relatives. If a
man is lucky, then, he will grow lots
of crops the following year. This is
how we also pray to Kookopölö.

kiy aw nime' pu' pep kya pi yanhaqam sinomuy aw tuu'awvaqw pu'
hak sakine' pu' aapiy yasmiq a'ni
hiihiita aniwnangwu. Yan it piw itam
Kookopölöt aw naawakinwisa.

Additional attributes that distinguish the Kookopölö kachina are two
hand-held objects, a rattle and a cane or crookstaff. The crookstaff, known as
ngölöshoya in the Third Mesa dialect, is an important item in the inventory of
Hopi ritual paraphernalia (Wright 1979: 92–94). Ceremonially also referred to
as *wukwtuvoyla*, "old age marker," it symbolizes longevity. According to Emory Sekaquaptewa (1995: personal communication), in former days the crook
was erected on top of the Taw kiva at the close of the Soyal ceremony. All
villagers then went there to grasp the crook and pray for a long life without
suffering. Kabotie (1977: 271) reports that on Second Mesa, where the item is
called *ngölökpi*, the cane had feathers attached signifying "the breath of life."
According to him, the crookstaff "represents the stages of life—from the
straight-backed vigor of youth to the bent shoulders of old age." Indirectly,
the attribute of the crookstaff characterizes Kookopölö as an old man, as Text
15 implies.

Text 15

Kookopölö katsina pay pi aaya'ytangwu. Pu' piw put yawnumgnwu,
ngölöshoyat. Put akw pay nanatöng-
tinumngwu. Pu' pay ephaqam piw
aw salavi pu' ngömaapi somiwtaqat
put pam yawtangwu. Pay hintiqw pi
pam oovi put tuwat yawtangwu. Sen
pi pam wuutaqaniiqe oovi pay pi
himuwa wuutaqanen pu' pay hiita
koho'ytangwu.

Kookopölö has a rattle. He also carries a cane. This he uses to prop himself up as he walks about. Once in a
while Douglas fir and juniper leaves
are tied to it. Who knows why he
carries this cane. Maybe because he is
an old man. For when one is old, one
needs a cane.

Kookopölö never has a flute, a fact that is reiterated in the literature and is also evident from all early visual renditions of the god (Washburn 1980: 124 n. 45; Hartmann 1978: fig. 16; Fewkes 1903: plate 25). Mails (1983: 176) is the only one who, in an illustration of his own, depicts the kachina holding a flute— obviously a distortion of Hopi cultural reality. More recently, Hopi carvers have begun to commercially fashion Kookopölö figurines with flutes. A good example is shown in a photograph by Teiwes (1991: 118). It pictures Lowell Talashoma sculpting "a Kookopölö, a Humpbacked Fluteplayer kachina doll," in "classic" Hohokam stance holding a flute whose distal part is shaped into a hemispherical end. Talashoma is a good example of how the vicious circle of acculturation has been closed, for, no longer familiar with their own traditions, Hopis have begun to use and accept the linkage of Kookopölö and the hump- backed fluteplayer as "culturally accurate."

Mention must also be made in this context of Martineau's (1973: 53) prop- osition that "the symbol of flute playing … was an almost universal method of depicting courting activities." Attempting to correct the erroneous notion that "the figure of the packman with a flute" is often labelled "Kokopelli, the hunchbacked Hopi deity known for his flute playing," he suggests that "flutes were commonly used in playing love songs in the hope of enticing a pretty girl into marriage." While this claim may be true in several Native American cul- tures, it must be pointed out that there is absolutely no ethnographic evidence nor any hint in the entire corpus of recorded Hopi oral literature that Hopis ever used flutes in courting. Nor is there, for that matter, a single love song in existence that Hopis could cite. This total lack of love songs in Hopi culture is a remarkable phenomenon considering the fact that songs are sung in a varie- ty of other situations, both secular and ceremonial.

In addition to supporting himself by means of the cane, Kookopölö also has another use for it. The latter clearly reveals the god's interest in the female sex, as may be gathered from Texts 16 and 17.

Text 16

Pu' pay Kookopölö haqam maanat yaw akw langaknangwu. Pay naami	Kookopölö will also employ it [the crookstaff] to pull a girl unto himself.

langaknangwu. Pay kitota piiwu. Put pam yaw pan ngung'api'yta.
Pu' piw put ngölöshoyat himuwa taaqa kanelvokmu'ytaqa naawakne' pu' pay put Kookopölöt nawkye' pay akw kanelhoymuy, mamngyatuy ngung'angwu.

That's what people also say. The crookstaff serves him to catch something.
Whenever a man who owns sheep wants that crookstaff, he may take it away from Kookopölö. He can then grab his little sheep and lambs with it.

Text 17

Pam Kookopölö pi pay put ngölös-hoyat akw hiita wiwaknangwuniiqe oovi put piw yawnumngwu. Akw naami hiita langaknangwu. Pu' momoymuy aw ngöytiwe' pay akw hiitawat ephaqam wiwaknangwu. Pu' piw put ngölöshoyay akw tuu-pevut söngne' pantaqat oomiq iitsi'ytangwu. Pu' aqw yottotangwu. Noq qa iits nawkiyangwu.

Kookopölö makes it a habit to rope things with his cane. That's the reason he carries it around. He pulls things over into his reach. For instance, when he engages in the *ngöytiw* [chasing game] with the women, he occasionally pulls one of them over to himself. Then again, he attaches some baked sweet corn to the tip of his cane and holds it up in the air. When the women then grab for it, they can't take it away so quickly.

Kookopölö and Fertility

Kookopölö is a "phallic deity" as Fewkes (1898: 663 n. 4) correctly states, although he admits (1903: 86) personally never to have seen the kachina in action. Smith (1952: 299) calls the god "one of the few ostentatiously porno-graphic impersonations among the Hopi, always portrayed with ... an erect phallus." Dockstader (1954: 123) suggests the kachina to be "the nearest equiv-alent to the physical aspects of sex." Grant (1967: 60), in less direct fashion, refers to him as "god-impersonator dressed with prominent erotic costume-details." Titiev (1939: 95–96), in summing up the field notes of Eggan, who, in 1934, was privileged to participate in a Kookopölö night dance at the Second Mesa village of Mishongnovi, describes the impersonators as follows: "Every performer had a hump fixed on his shoulders, and a large red 'penis' (of gourd?) strapped in position over the underwear. Each dancer carried a rattle in one hand and held his 'penis' with the other throughout the performance. As they entered the kiva the katcinas lunged at the spectators, particularly at the women. They sang and danced facing the audience, advancing in unison occasionally and singing a slow song. The spectators laughed hilariously." Whether the artist in Fewkes's compilation of Hopi kachinas (1903: plate 25) depicts Kookopölö with a natural penis, as Dockstader (1954: 123) surmises, or whether he is "wearing a large artificial phallus, commonly made from a gourd or carved of wood," is not clear from the illustration.[3] Parsons (1926: 206 n. 3) insists that he has a gourd penis.

However, this is not the issue. Crucial in this context is Smith's observation that Kookopölö's penis is erect. Since Hopis, in former days, were much more comfortable with the naked human body than was the white society—Hopi children, for example, went naked for many years—the simple phallic representation of the penis would be without special significance. Ithyphallic portrayals, on the other hand, do symbolize procreative power and sexual renewal. This also seems to be borne out in rock art images of anthropomorphic figures. Figures with phallic appendages simply mark gender; ithyphallic ones, on the other hand, express reproduction and fertility.

Due to the early influence of missionaries concerned about public decency and morality, and because of "restraints imposed by the American government on all erotic and phallic exhibitions" (Titiev 1939: 98), ithyphallic appearances of the god Kookopölö are now a thing of the past. This and other observations relating to Kookopölö's tumescent organ may be gathered from Texts 18 and 19.

---

3. For evidence from the oral literature for carved cottonwood dildos, see Malotki 1983b: 212.

Text 18

Pam pay as hisat yaw siipoq qa tupki'ytangwu. Pay kwasi'at angqw
haayiwtangwu yaw hisat. Noq pu' pi
pay ima Pahaanam pi yesqw pay pu'
oovi Kookopölö qa pankyangw pitungwu. Pay pitunik pay aqw tupki'y-
tangwu. Noq hisat Kookopölö pi pay
kwasiy yaw maatakni'ytangwuniiqe
oovi pam yaw hakiy pas suutsopni-
qey oovi qa pitkuntangwu. Pu' it pi
yan yu'a'atota. Noq pay nu' qa hisat
pu' hayphaqam put haqam aw yori.

Antsa pi pay pas suruy, pas
kwasiy, maatakni'ytangwu. Pu'
hayphaqam pam Kookopölö piptuqa
pam pay mit pay paakot angqw
yukiwtaqat kwasi'yta. Put pay siipoq
oovi somi'yta. Pay pi puma pi aatöqe
kwasi'yyungngwuniqw pay put pu'
puma qa maatakni'yyungngwu. Pay
piw put kwasit naap yukiwtaqat pay
qa put hintsatskyangwu puma puu'.

People say that in the old days Kookopölö did not cover up his crotch.
His penis was there hanging down.
But ever since the whites settled here,
he does not appear like that anymore.
Whenever he wants to come, he covers up his loins. Way back he openly
showed his organ. He wore no kilt so
that he could have intercourse with a
woman without delay. This is what
people say. I myself have never seen
a Kookopölö like this in recent times.

It is really true that Kookopölö
used to show his real tail or penis.
More recently, whenever he made an
appearance, he wore a penis carved
out of cottonwood, which was tied to
his crotch. Underneath was his real
penis, which nowadays he dares not
show anymore. This self-made penis,
too, is no longer seen today.

Text 19

Hisat antsa pi pay i' Hopi pi tuwat
Kookopölöt akw it imuy tsaatsakw-
muy tuwat wuuhaqlawqw oovi pam
Kookopölö antsa hisat pite' susmataq
kwasi'ytangwu. Pu' kwasiy ngu'y-
numngwu. Pankyangw pu' himuwa
aw naawaknaqw pu' awnen antsa

Long ago, it is true, the Hopi used to
increase the number of his offspring
with the help of Kookopölö. Therefore, way back Kookopölö used to
come with his penis clearly visible.
He was going around holding his
penis. In this way, when a woman

kwasiy horokne' qa pas pi pas löwa-
miq kwasiy panangwu. Pay naap
haqaqw pam yomimiykungwu, put
kwasit akwa.
   Yanhaqam i' antsa hiniwtiqw
pu' antsa Pahaanam öki. Noq pu'
puma put pan kwasiy maatakni'y-
kyangw piw qa yuwsi'ytaqw qa
himuyangwu. Noq oovi pu' pay
Kookopölö yuwsi'ytangwu. Putakw
naatupki'ytangwu. Pu' hisat pay as
piw pantangwu yawi. Pay naat qa
pas pas hisat, pay pu' hayphaqam
pay yuwsi'ykyangw pay kwasiy
horoknangwu as piw. Nen pu' pay
nuutumi maataknat pu' pay ahoy
aatöqehovinapnay aqw tupkyangwu.
Noq hisat pi oovi pas as pam susmataq kwasi'ynumngwu.

prayed to him, he stepped up to her,
took his penis, but did not really
insert it into her vagina. He would
simply carry out some quick pelvic
thrusts from whatever side of the
woman he happened to be standing
on.
   This is how things used to happen when the whites arrived. They
did not like Kookopölö showing his
penis and appearing without clothes.
That's why nowadays he is clothed.
He covers up his nakedness. Now
this was long ago. In more recent
times he already wore clothes, but
used to take out his penis. Upon
showing it to the people, he hid it in
his underpants again. Way back,
however, he used to go around stark
naked.

While it is true that Kookopölö no longer appears ithyphallically, displays
of mock copulation can routinely be observed, both by him and Kokopölmana,
his female counterpart (see Texts 22 and 36 below). Grant's (1967: 61) observation that "the god-impersonators dressed with prominent erotic costume-
details ... proved too earthy for the tourists" and that, for this reason, "the gay
couple appear rarely and in a thoroughly censored routine" is therefore an
overstatement. Nor must such acts of simulated intercourse be interpreted as
"libidinous" (Brill 1984: 17), "pornographic" (Smith 1952: 299), or "lewd and
obscene" (Titiev 1939: 98). Ritual intercourse as practiced by Kookopölö was
never objectionable in the eyes of the Hopi. Rather, it must be seen as a gesture
of deep symbolic significance, an affirmation of the need to generate human
life, thereby assuring the very existence and ultimately survival of the Hopi
people. As Dockstader (1954: 123) correctly remarks,

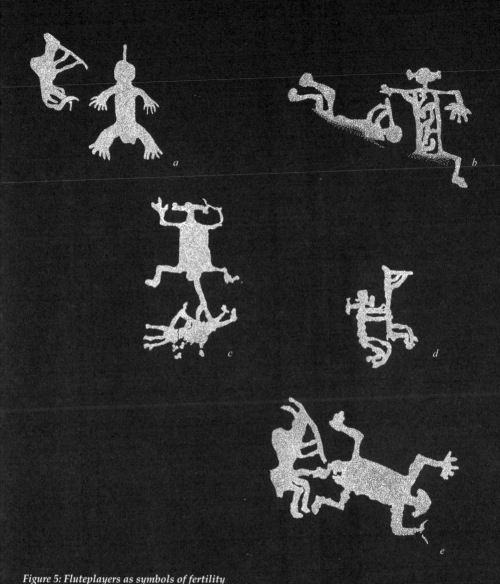

Figure 5: Fluteplayers as symbols of fertility
*Fluteplayer images occur in scenes with fertility themes as indicated by the
actual depiction of copulation (c, e), as well as the proximal association of specifically identified male and female figures (a, b, d). In virtually all cases the fluteplayer is depicted as a male, while his partner is clearly marked female, by
the presence of either women's hair whorls (b, c, d) or explicit female anatomical
features (a, c, e). This emphasis on fertility appears to be late and is most pronounced
in the Rio Grande River Valley area.*

insistence by the Whites on adoption of a new way of life by the Hopis in the field of morals has placed an increasingly unhealthy emphasis upon sex. Whereas those rites which were accompanied by expressions of sexual activity were presumably once viewed naturally, today there is a tendency toward conscious obscenity, in an attempt to shock or insult White visitors. This unfortunate gesture has, of course, provided ammunition for those who would put an end to all native ceremonials.

It is difficult to say to what degree White contact has affected the activities of Kókopölö Kachina. Certainly there seems to be a greater tendency to regard the impersonation as amusing and as giving opportunity to embarrass White spectators than to consider the fertility aspect. The increased consciousness of sex—certainly traceable to White contact—has not only affected the fundamental philosophy of Kókopölö (and, therefore, the basic reasons for his appearance in the Kachina cycle) but has had an even more marked influence upon his conduct.

Still, the primary role of Kookopölö as a manifestation of human fertility is still apparent to the Hopi when consulted about the god's behavior. Leigh Jenkins (in Widdison 1991: 57), confirms this, adding that, more specifically, the kachina "represents the rejuvenation of life." My own recorded field notes amply corroborate the fertility of Kookopölö, as is readily evident not only from a Kookopölö song (Text 20), but also from Texts 21, 22, and 23.

Text 20

Ayaha, iyihiiyiihi.	Ayaha, iyihiiyiihi.
Kookopölölö, Kookopölölö.	Kookopölö, Kookopölö.
Wuutaqa, wuutaqa.	Old man, old man,
Pam niikyango	But still
Momoymuy amuupa	He keeps jumping up and down
tso'o'otinumngwu.	among the women.
Yaw pam qatsiyamuy	They say to make their lives grow

wungwintaniqeyu
Oovi pumuy amuupa
tso'o'otinumngwu.
Yanhaqam itam titwi'yyungwa.
Aha'ihi hiiyi, hiiyi, hiiyi.

He is jumping up and down
among them.
This is how we know to dance.
Aha'ihi hiiyi, hiiyi, hiiyi.

Text 21

Kookopölö pi pay nuutum pay pitungwu. Pu' paasat pam pay qa pas
momoymuy pas hintsanngwu. Pay
mavoktat tso'o'oykungwu. Ephaqam
mongaqwwatningwu, pu' ephaqam
pay aakwayngyangaqw momiq
mavoktat pu' pay yantingwu, aw
tso'o'oykungwu. Pay yaw pan pam
piw pumuy amungem tihut yuyku-
qat pay kitotangwu.

Whenever Kookopölö comes along
with other kachinas, he does not
really have intercourse with the
women. He just embraces them and
starts to jump up and down. Once in
a while he will do so embracing a
woman from the front, occasionally
also from behind. People say that in
this fashion he is making a child for
them.

Text 22

Pam antsa Powamuyve pitungwu.
Nen pu' pam qa momoymuy ngöynumngwu. I' himuwa wuuti sen pi
maana pay as kongtat qa tiite' pu'
put aw nakwsungwu. Aw nakwse'
pu' aw hoomay oyangwu. Nen pu'
aw pangqawngwu, "Ta'a, nu'
tinawakna. Nu' qa tiitaqe uumi
naawaknaqw pu' um nuy hin yukunaqw pu' sen nu' tiitani," himuwa
aw kitangwu.

    Paasat pu' Kookopölö put suma-
vokte' pu' aqw yomimitangwu, tsop-
lawngwu. Pan pam pantsakmangwu

It is true that Kookopölö comes during the Powamuy ceremony. On that
occasion he does not chase women.
Instead, any woman or girl who just
got married and has not given birth
yet goes up to him. Upon doing so
she offers him sacred cornmeal. Then
she usually says, "All right, I desire a
child. Because I have not borne a
child yet, I'm praying to you that you
can do something to me that I may
have a child."

    Kookopölö quickly embraces her
and thrusts his hips into her a few

tuwat Powamuyve. Pu' ephaqam su-'an hiitawat yukunaqw pu' himuwa antsa nö'yilte' pu' tiitangwu. Yan it piw put Kookopölöt aw naanawak-nangwu, ima momoyam, mamant.

times. He has intercourse with her. That's what he typically does during the Powamuy ceremony. Once in a while, when he succeeds with a woman, she really gets pregnant and gives birth to a child. In this manner married and unmarried women pray to Kookopölö.

Text 23

Hopimomoyam pay piw Kookopölöt aw tihut oovi naanawaknangwu. Put aw hoomay akw pay tuuvinglalwa-ngwu okiw. Pay ephaqam himuwa pas antsa tinawakne' pu' paasat Koo-kopölöt aw wuuti naakuwaatingwu. Pu' pam put tsopngwu. Pan yaw peetu haqawat momoyam timkiwya, tihut naanawaknaqam. Pay pi son wuuti naap haqam aw naakuwaati-ngwu. Pay qa hak haqamniqw paasat pu' pam put aw naakuwaatingwu, Kookopölöt awi.

Hopi women pray to Kookopölö for offspring. As always, they use sacred cornmeal when they pray. Occasion-ally, when a woman really desires a child, she will offer herself to Kooko-pölö. He then has intercourse with her. In this manner some women who are anxious to have offspring are given children. Of course, the woman does not offer herself to the kachina in just any place. Usually she does so when no one else is around.

As was pointed out already, Kookopölö's acts of publicly performed intercourse are completely mimetic in nature. For this reason, the kachina has survived into modern times. Another Hopi fertility god, the Mastopkatsina, "Mastop kachina," did not fare equally well. He has long since disappeared, for his sexual interaction with women, especially those who attempted to escape him or those who thought they were barren, was on occasion more than symbolic. Because of this important difference between Kookopölö and Mastopkatsina, Text 24 is included here.

Text 24

Pam pi pay qa pas hakiy aqw yomi-miykungwu, Mastopkatsina. Pam pi pay hakiy sukyaktsimi nan'ivo matyawt pu' tso'o'oykungwu. Pay pansa pam ang nuutuupa pannumngwu. Pu' niikyangw hak yaw waayaqw pu' pam hakiy ngöyve' pu' pam pas hakiy angk kiiyat aw pakiqw pu' pam angk pakye' paasat pu' pam pas hakiy tsopngwu. Oovi hakim pumuy pan ang pannumyaqw hak qa waayangwu, maana, wuuti.

   Puma hisat Soyalangwuy ep, payistalqwhaqam puma pangqw lööyöm yamakngwu, yangqw Kwankivangaqw. Pu' momoyam pay naap haqaqw pay tiitimayyangwuniqw pu' puma pay pangqw yamakye' pu' pay puma momoymuy aqw warikt pu' hiitawat aakwayngyangaqw tso-'o'oykungwu. Pu' himuwa tinawakne' pumuy awningwu. Pam pay naap awningwu. Pay pam haqami kiiyat awniqat aw pangqawqw pu' pam put tsopngwu, katsina. Pu' pay pam pas antsa tinawaknaqw pu' pam pay put pantingwu.

The Mastop kachina does not make pelvic thrusts at a female. Instead, he places his hands on both of her shoulders and then starts jumping up and down. That's the only way he carries on among the women. However, if a female runs away from him, he chases her, and if she seeks refuge in a house, follows her and then really has intercourse with her. For this reason, a girl or woman is not supposed to run away when the Mastop kachinas are about.

   In the old days it was always on the third day of the Soyal ceremony that two Mastop kachinas emerged from the kiva, usually from the Kwan kiva. Women were watching the dance, of course, from all sorts of places. So after the two kachinas emerged from that kiva, they dashed toward the women and starting their jumping up and down behind whichever female they chose. Whenever a woman wanted a child, she would approach the kachinas on her own and, after telling one of them which house to enter, the Mastop kachina then had intercourse with her. That's what a female did if she truly desired offspring.

Kookopölö as a powerful embodiment of generative potency and vigor is also evident from the oral literature. In "The Man-Crazed Woman," the Kookopölö origin legend included in part 2, barren women desirous of children seek the god out of their own free will. In "The Two Kokopöl Boys" the two protagonists are charged with sexuality. To be sure, the circumstances in which Kookopölö displays his superior sexual knowledge are sometimes embedded in humorous scenarios, and in these he has all the hallmarks of a trickster, as Wellmann (1974: 4) has pointed out. But this fact does not diminish his function as fertility figure. An excellent example to what extent this potency has been reanalyzed in recent times is one of Montoya's renderings of "Kokopelli" (Hill 1995: 40) in which sexual potency is symbolized not by a tumescent phallus but by a pottery bowl with a Zia rain bird motif on it.

The sexual charge Kookopölö embodies seems to extend even to the *tihu*, "kachina doll," that is carved in his likeness. (*Tihu* literally denotes "child," and not "doll," though "doll" is now the commonly established term.) As I have pointed out elsewhere (Malotki 1991: 58), the association of these carved figurines with fertility was once the reason for the Hopi taboo not to sell them. As toys or playthings for young uninitiated girls, the Kookopölö *tihu* had especially strong undercurrents of fertility. An episode characterized as a "curious instance of prenatal influence" by Stephen (1936: 388–89) nicely documents this point. Worth mentioning in this connection is the fact that the *tihu* is bestowed not on a little girl, as is customary, but on a married woman who is already pregnant. Soon after she received the doll at the occasion of the Powamuy ceremony "her child was born, a boy, who almost as soon as born began to play with his penis. The child is now a little over a year old and he still constantly toys with the penis, the glans of which begins to look somewhat like distended rubber, the parents consider this a good omen of coming vigour."

From all evidence, the reason for the attraction that Kookopölö enjoys among the women is not limited to his sexual potency. He is also believed to be an industrious and productive farmer, a trait that contributes to the general halo of fertility and fecundity that surrounds him, both in the human and vegetal domain. Text 25 attests to Kookopölö's power of vegetal propagation.

Text 25

Kokopölö pas kya pi piw qa na'öna-
ningwu. Niiqe oovi hin'ur hiita aniwnangwu. Soosoyam navoti'yyungwa
pam himu pay hiita hin'ur a'aniwnangwu. Noq oovi piw pay mamant
piw pas put naanawaknangwuqat
kitotangwu. Pay yaw tuwat manson-
veningwu.

Kookopölö is supposed to be very
industrious. Therefore he grows large
quantities of crops. Everybody
knows that. People say that for this
reason the unmarried girls really
want him. He in turn is always
surrounded by girls.

Public appearances of the fertility god occur in a variety of contexts. He
will either come alone, that is, as an individual figure, or in a whole group of
lookalikes. In the latter mode, an entire dance formation of Kookopölös will go
from kiva to kiva and entertain the various audiences at the occasion of a
mihikqwtikive, "kachina night dance." However, public plaza dances also seem
to occur. As a solitary figure, on the other hand, he is either one of the many
personages that make up the *qöqöntinumya*, "kachina procession," during the
Powamuy ceremony, or he participates in a dance of Soyohömkatsinam,
"Mixed kachinas." Texts 26 and 27 illustrate the last-named practices.

Text 26

I' Kookopölö, pam pay pi naap hisat
pitungwu, imuy Soyohömkatsinmuy
amumum. Pu' piw Powamuyve katsinam ökiqw ephaqam amumum
pitungwu. Antsa qöqöntinumyaqw
ep piw amumum pitungwu.

Kookopölö will come just at any
time, usually with a group of Mixed
kachinas. Also, when the kachinas
come during the Powamuy ceremony, he accompanies them once in a
while. Especially, when the kachinas
parade through the village, he is
there also.

Text 27

Pu' ephaqam pay pam Kookopölö
pay suukyaninik pay pi pumuy
mimuy Soyohömkatsinmuy amu-

Occasionally, a Kookopölö wants to
come by himself. He then usually
accompanies a group of Mixed kachi-

mumningwu. Puma pi pay hiihii-
tuyangwu. Namiqriwtangwuniqw
pay ephaqam pi pay suukya pumuy
amumum pitungwu. Nen pu' pay
kivaapeq pay pan lööqmuy amumi
ngöytiwt pu' pay wunimangwu. Pu'
yamaktokyangw piw pay antingwu.
Pay pam qa pas piw teevep ngöytiw-
lawngwu.

　Ephaqam Soyohömkatsinam
talö'tikive'yyungwniniqw pu' pam
Kookopölö amumumnen kiisonmi
ökye', leetsiltiqw pay tuwat angqe'
ngöytiwnumngwu momoymuy
amuupa. Pu' tiivantivaqw pu' piw
nuutum wunimantivangwu.

nas. These can be all sorts of different
types. Since they are all mixed up,
once in while a Kookopölö is also
among them. Upon entering the kiva,
he first allows himself to be chased
by a couple of women before he joins
in the dance. As the group exits the
kiva, he does the same. But he does
not engage in the *ngöytiw* [gift-
snatching game] all the time.

　Once in while, when Mixed
kachinas stage a plaza performance
during the day, Kookopölö comes
with them to the plaza. While the
other kachinas line up, he plays
ngöytiw with the women. As soon as
the kachinas begin to dance, however, he also starts dancing.

　Individually, Kookopölö may also accompany any of the Kipokkatsinam,
"Raider kachinas." They typically make their entry at the conclusion of a public kachina dance to punish—that is, purify—the clowns for their licentious
behavior during the sacred ceremony. As the Raider kachinas fall upon the
frantic clowns who are trying to escape their punishers, Kookopölö does his
name "robber fly" justice as he pounces on them.

Text 28

Pu' pay ephaqam mimuy Kipokka-
tsinmuy amumum piw pitungwu.

Occasionally, Kookopölö also comes
with the Raider kachinas.

　The behavior and antics of entire Kookopölö groups are documented in
Texts 29, 30, and 31. Note in particular the custom of *ngöytiw* that all of them
allude to. This "chasing game" or "gift-snatching game," which, according to

46   *Kokopelli*

Titiev (1939: 94 n. 11) once also could be observed after the Tsu', "Snake," or Len, "Flute," ceremonies between ordinary men and women, casts Kookopölö in the role of the trickster again. The ancient game, which was marked by certain elements of erotic play, is performed in a sexually rather explicit and dramatic manner in the tale "The Two Kokopöl Boys" (Malotki 1995: 65–97). Originally, the male tempter or teaser in the game seems to have used flowers and, later, edible greens. Today, mostly store-bought items are preferred, including cookie sheets and rolls of toilet paper.

Text 29

Pu' pay ephaqamtiqw pay pumasa piw katsinam ökingwu. Pay puma wuuhaqniiqam ökingwu, Kookopölt, mihikqwtikive. Pay taalö' piw ephaqam. Mihikqw tiikive puma piw yungiwma. Tuupevut na'mangwu'yvaya. Pu' pay put piw mokiwyay pi pay ngöytiwngwu, tuuvimoq momoymuy aqw. Qa iits nawkingwu himuwaniqw pay aw tututsiwngwu. Kiisonve pay piw pantotingwu, puma Kookopölt. Pay Kookopölt tiive' pay hihin kunalalwaqw amumi tsutsuyngwu sumataq.

Once in a great while a large group of Kookopölö kachinas comes during a night dance. Occasionally, also during the day. At the night dance they go from kiva to kiva, bringing baked sweet corn as gifts. With their little bundles they invite the women, who are seated on the upper kiva floor, to do the *ngöytiw* with them. If a woman fails to take the held-out item away quickly, Kookopölö ridicules her. On the plaza, the Kookopölös carry on likewise. Whenever they perform a dance, they act funny. As a result, people laugh at them.

Text 30

Pay pi hisat Kookopöltsa tiiva. Niiqe pay naat puma qa tiivantivaqw pu' peetu pay mamantuy ang amuupa ngöytiwlalwa. Tukyamsit wuuhaq sitkoyaqe pay puma putsa ngöytiwya. Pay naap hisatniqw haqam

Once groups of Kookopölö kachinas used to dance by themselves. Before they started, some of them had themselves chased around by the women in *ngöytiw*. As a rule, they picked a lot of larkspur, which they held out

Kookopölö maanat, wuutit aw pite'
pay pi aw ngöytiwngwu. Pu' hak put
nawkingwu. Pu' pi pay lemoktuk-
tangat, kentit, puuvut pi pu' ngöy-
tiwyangwu. Noq hisat pu' pay pam
kya pi sihutsa pi ngöytiwngwu. Pu'
hiita mit son pi qee, totonat. Pu' pay
pasipnat piw somte' pay piw putni-
ngwu.

as a prize. Whenever a Kookopölö
approached a girl or woman, he
would tease her with these flowers.
Then someone wrestled them away
from him. Nowadays, the kachinas
also use boxes of Cracker Jacks,
candy, and such things to invite the
women to chase them. In the old
days, however, they only used flowers. And of course, *totona* [a carrot-
like root]. Or they tied *pasipna* [the
sweet roots of a legume] into bunches
and used them in *ngöytiw*.

Text 31

Pam pay naap hisat pite' pam momoymuy amuupa ngöytiwtinum-
ngwu. Oovi piw kur pam nuutum
Soyohömkatsinmuy amumumniqw
pu' puma kivamiq mihikqw yungiw-
wisngwu, katsinam. Noq pay momoyam pi tuuwingaqw yesngwu
tiitimayye'. Pu' pay Kookopölö
pakye' hiitawat pay qatuwtaqat aw
ngöwtiwngwu. Pam pi pay hiita
mooki'ytangwu, tuupevu'ewakw,
hiita na'mangwuy. Pay pam pan
hiitawat aw tongokye' pay tsaakw
yukuuqey unangwtingwu.

Whenever Kookopölö comes—and
he may come at just about any time—
he goes around among the women
engaging them in *ngöytiw*. He holds
out a gift to them which they attempt
to wrestle from him. And so he will
also be in a group of Soyohömkatsinam [Mixed kachinas] when
they visit the various kivas during a
night dance. The females are traditionally seated on the upper platform
of the kiva. As soon as Kookopölö
enters, he entices one of them into
ngöytiw, extending in his hand a
wrapped-up gift like baked sweet
corn or other presents. If in doing so
he touches the female, he feels as if
he has fathered a child.

Texts 32 and 33 characterize the typical night dance behavior of a Kookopölö group. The painting by Kabotie (1977: 90) gives a vivid impression of the dance formation.

Text 32

Puma pi pay piw ökingwu, Kookopölt. Pay wuuhaqniiqamye' pay yan leetsiwkyangw puma pi pay oovi suusus tiivangwu. Pay yanhaqam pay hintsatskyangwu puma. Momiqwat pay yoktotangwu. Puma qa naanangk namtötötangwu. Pay momiqwatsa yan taykyaakyangwyangwu.

Whenever a large group of Kookopölö kachinas comes, they line up [abreast] and dance very slowly. That's how they usually perform. They all stoop forward and never turn around, one after the other. They are always facing forward while they dance.

Text 33

Pay tiivaqe pay hiita suususniiqat akw tiikive'yyungngwu. Pay kunalalwangwu. I' pööla'ytaqa ngölöshoyat yawnumngwu. Put akw naatöngnumngwu, ispi pam wuutaqaniikyangw pööla'ytaqe oovi. Aw nahongvitime' qa munukniqey oovi put akw naatöngnumngwu.

When Kookopölös dance in a group, they always have a slow song. They are quite funny actually. Each humpbacked kachina carries a cane that he uses to prop himself up with. After all, he's an old man and has a hump. He puts pressure on this cane and leans on it in order to keep from tripping.

Before concluding this chapter on Kookopölö, one curious ethnographic fact must be mentioned that, to date, has not received any attention in the literature. In addition to the well-known hunchbacked deity of Kookopölö, there exists a Hopi kachina, Taawakopö, that is based on Kookopölö yet has a radically different appearance. Taawakopö is named for his mask, which resembles that of Taawakatsina, the "Sun kachina," and for *kopö*, the alternate name for *kookopölö*, the robber or assassin fly. Besides his different mask,

Plate 1. Known as *kookopölö* by the Hopis, the robber fly is an aggressive predator that sucks the bodily fluids out of its trapped prey. Distinguished by a very prominent hump, the insect is the natural model for the Kookopölö kachina, commonly misspelled Kokopelli.

Robber flies are persistent copulators. The fact that they are often encountered in copula may have given rise to the overriding roles of encouraging reproduction and fertility that the Hopis associate with the male Kookopölö and the female Kokopölmana kachinas. Photo courtesy of Robert Lavigne.

Plate 2. Among the largest of plant-sucking insects and noted for their loud buzzing sounds, cicadas are equipped with a proboscis that, in the eyes of the Hopis, resembles a flute. Music from this flute is believed to cause the hot weather vital for the growth and maturation of Hopi crops. For this reason, they see the cicada as the model for the many fluteplayer depictions found in the rock art of the American Southwest.

Plates 3–5. This sequence of images illustrates the shift in cultural conceptualization that has affected the Hopi kachinas Kookopölö and Kokopölmana. In the first picture, a painting from the late 1890s (Fewkes 1903: Plate XXV), Kookopölö is depicted ithyphallically to characterize the god's generative potency. In the second picture, a kachina doll from the 1950s (courtesy of Museum of Northern Arizona, Catalog No. 897), Kookopölö's phallus, generally depicted in the form of a painted gourd, has disappeared due to pressure from the dominant white society that considered the open display of genitalia obscene. While in these two illustrations, the male figure clearly—and correctly—lacks a flute, the carving in the third picture from the late 1990s (courtesy of Cameron Trading Post) shows Kookopölö playing a flute as a result of a mistaken identification with the fluteplayer motif in Southwestern rock art iconography. Note also that while Kookopölö's once overt sexual aspects have completely disappeared, overtones of sexuality are now noticeable in his female partner Kokopölmana.

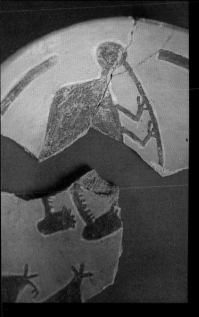

Plate 6. Homol'ovi Polychrome bowl from Nuvakwewtaqa (Chavez Pass), northern Arizona. Smithsonian Institutions Collections USNM Catalog No. 157573. Photograph courtesy of Peter J. Pilles, Jr., Coconino National Forest.

Plate 7. Sikyatki Polychrome bowl from Awat'ovi. Courtesy of Museum für Völkerkunde, Berlin (Germany), Catalog No. IV B 3252. Note the ithyphallic portrayal of the two fluteplayers. Damaged during World War II, the lower end of the vessel has been restored. Only eight of the original thirteen ithyphallic dancers remain.

Plate 8. Easy recognition of the motif and fascination with the instrument and its music may explain why the motif has become so popular in our culture. East of Bluff, Utah.

Plate 9. Although the participants in this intercourse scene have some distinct non-human traits, scenes of this kind have undoubtedly fostered the common assumption that the fluteplayer is linked to human procreation. North of Flagstaff, Arizona.

Plate 10. Uncharacteristically, this large fluteplayer is pot-bellied rather than humpbacked. To enhance its visibility, it was chalked by vandals. East of Gallup, New Mexico.

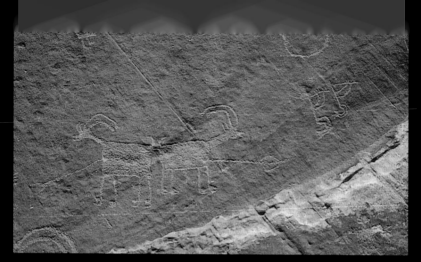

Plate 11. Dating to late Basketmaker times (approx. A. D. 700), these twinned stick-figure fluteplayers are believed to be among the earliest attested of the motif. Note how they compliment the paired bighorn sheep depiction. Near Kayenta, Arizona.

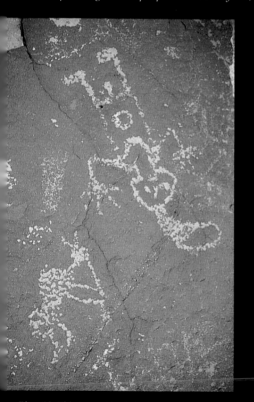

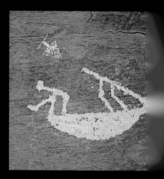

Plate 12. Elements associated wi[t] ticular fluteplayer may provide c[...] to its cultural function. However [...] case, the significance of the proje[c...] point aimed directly at the flute r[...] a mystery. Near Winslow, Arizor[...]

Plate 13. This insect-like fluteplayer with a segmented body and antennae next to an upside-down or falling anthropomorph may be suggestive of shamanic flight or a ritual related to death. North of Santa Fe, New Mexico.

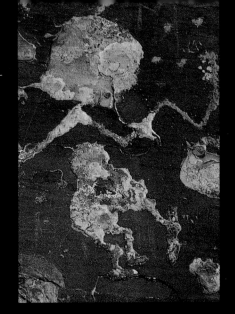

Plate 14. The fluteplayer, one of the Southwest's most widely known rock art motifs, has a simple but distinctive morphology that makes it easily recognizable even when heavily spalled, as in this case. East of Holbrook, Arizona.

Plate 15. Overwhelmingly, fluteplayers have human characteristics, but animal, insect, and composite (part human, part animal) figures also occur. This one appears to be an armadillo. North of Santa Fe, New Mexico.

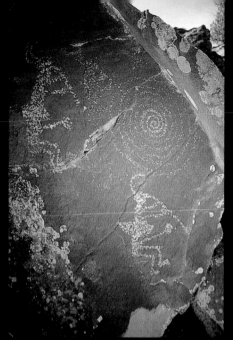

Plate 16. Assuming that the three fluteplayers surrounding the large spiral are the work of a single artist, one wonders why he chose to portray them so differently and what the significance was of the unusual midriff elements in two of them. North of Santa Fe, New Mexico.

Plate 17. For some reason, the artist who created this panel felt compelled to add the fluteplayer symbol (left) to the dominating geometrics. We will never know why. Near Winslow, Arizona.

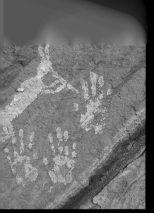

Plate 18. This simple juxtaposition of the ubiquitous fluteplayer with the highly personal handprints is strikingly appealing, giving the impression that the viewer is in the presence of the ancient artist. Near Chinle, Arizona.

Plate 19. Multiple-image panels like this one often make it difficult or even impossible to determine the actual role of the fluteplayer. East of Cameron, Arizona.

...nel stands out through its fluid anthropomorphs. Note how the wildly animated ...ests sharply with the more conventional one on its left. Near Chinle, Arizona.

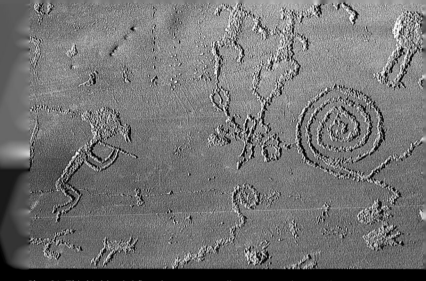

Plate 21. This bird-headed fluteplayer may actually represent a shaman. Shamans claim to chang[e] [i]nto birds to journey from the real to the spirit world in the sky. Near Holbrook, Arizona.

Plate 22. Although m[ost] depicted singly, grou[ps] not uncommon. This [ ] their feather headdres[ses] humpbacked postures [ ] dancing musicians in [ ] Near Santa Fe, New [Mexico].

Plate 24. Painted fluteplayer images are much less common than engraved ones. This par-ticular example is unique because of its hyper-elongated flute. Near Sedona, Arizona.

Plate 25. This seated fluteplayer is an integral component of a long row of horned quadrupeds. Scenes such as this one are undoubtedly responsible for the "pied piper" interpretation attributed to the motif when occurring with game animals. East of Cameron, Arizona.

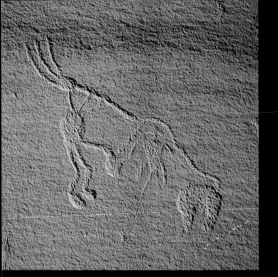

Plate 26. Scenes like this, laden with sexual imagery, including an oversized penis, a disembodied vulva, and a line linking the fluteplayer's penis with the vulva, have inspired Western notions of the fluteplayer as Casanova or Don Juan. Near Bluff, Utah.

Plate 27. This realistically engraved fluteplayer lacks the bent-knee posture and humped back generally attributed to the derivative Kokopelli icon. Note the necklaces, kilt, and sash that give the figure the air of flute-playing ritualist. Near Albuquerque, New Mexico.

Plate 28. In this unique portrayal a supine fluteplayer is carried on the head of a human figure. The adjacent elements may represent stylized participants in a ritualistic procession. North of Flagstaff, Arizona.

Plate 29. *The relatively small size of the fluteplayer in this panel—in comparison to the powerful "Mother of Game," serpent, and mythic archer—indicates that it played a minor role in the overall composition. Near Holbrook, Arizona.*

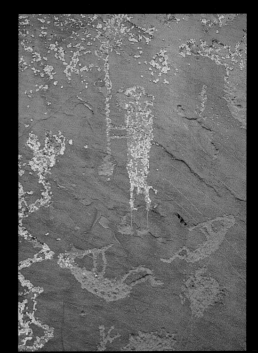

Plate 30. *The two reclining fluteplayers positioned at the feet of a staff bearer suggest the use of flutes in ritual activities centered around a powerful personage or shaman. Near Holbrook, Arizona.*

Plate 31. The grotesquely ithyphallic condition of these five stick-figure fluteplayers strongly suggests an association with human sexuality and procreation. Near Bluff, Utah.

Plate 32. In the eyes of the Hopi, the cicada is the natural model for the fluteplayer. Endowed with heat power, the insect thus becomes responsible for the sprouting and growth of plants. A similar belief may be portrayed here. Near Bluff, Utah.

Plate 33. This fluteplayer, with an extremely long flute, is clearly associated with a bighorn sheep, a context that suggests hunting magic. Near Winslow, Arizona.

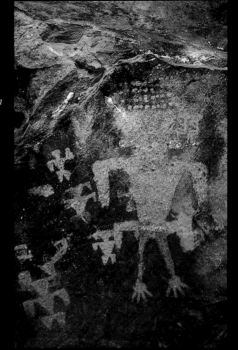

Plate 34. The two tiny fluteplayers in this scene appear to be subordinate to a much larger and more important figure, perhaps a supernatural being, in much the same way that small animal spirit helpers are often depicted assisting a much larger shaman figure. Near St. George, Utah.

Plate 35. The two fluteplayers in this complex petroglyphic assemblage are perhaps some of the earliest examples, dating to Basketmaker times, approximately A.D. 500–700. Monument Valley, Utah.

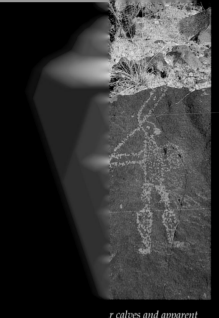

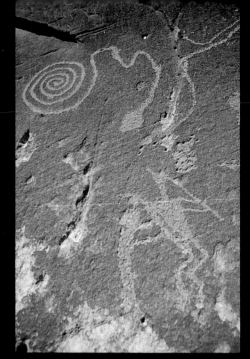

r calves and apparent
_ack, on this fluteplayer
_of a long-distance trader
_her fluteplayer images
_imilarly. North of
_.

Plate 37. Associated with serpents, these paired
fluteplayers may be symbolic of a water or rain-
making ritual. Near Moab, Utah.

Taawakopö also lacks a hump. In its stead, the kachina carries a *taawa'ikwilni,* "sunshield." Colton (1949: 36) reports a "Kuwan Kokopölö" (correctly, Kuwankokopölö) that is supposed to have a green face and a velvet shirt and white pants. There is no mention of a sunshield in his description, nor is the carved figurine labeled "Kuwan Kokopelli—Colored Assassin Fly Kachina" in Wright (1977: 116) equipped with this object. When comparing the latter with Erickson's "Tawa Kokopelli Kachina" (1977: 61), it becomes obvious that Colton's Kuwankokopölö may be synonymous with my Taawakopö.

In her attempts to explain the hump of Kookopölö, Brill (1984: 37), without being aware of the existence of the Taawakopö, suggests that "the back shield or tablet" observable in other Hopi and Zuni ceremonial figures "might have been conventionalized in prehistoric art forms into a hump." From all indications, it is the other way around: The "ugly" hump of Kookopölö was replaced in the prettified version of Taawakopö by the "colorfully beautiful" sunshield. The descriptive details of Taawakopö listed in Text 34 seems to refer exclusively to the Third Mesa variant of this kachina. An excellent specimen in the form of a carved *tihu* is available in the collection at the Museum of Northern Arizona, Flagstaff.

Text 34

Taawakopö pi piw pay as Kooko-pölöt an maatsiwkyangw pam pas lomave'ytangwu. Pam Taawat an tsöqa'asi'ytangwu. Pam oovi pas sakwapkuwkyangw oomiqwat qalpaqe sutsvoqwat sikyangpuniqw pu' sutsvoq paalangpuningwu, it taawayungyaput ani'. Pu' unangwpa pas powamuytsöqa'asi'ytangwu. Pam oovi pas lomahintangwu. Palamtsaput torikiwtangwu. Pu' mö-tsapngönkwewa'ytangwu, kweewat, pitkunat. Pu' lomahopitotstakyangw piw honhokyasmi'ytangwu. Pan pam

The Taawakopö is named like Koo-kopölö [*kopö* being an abbreviated form of *kookopölö*], but unlike the latter he is beautifully decorated. His body paint is like that of the Sun kachina. So, his countenance is blue-green, with the two divided segments along his forehead being yellow and red, just like in a wicker plaque showing the Sun. The chest is daubed like that of a Powamuy kachina. Taawakopö is therefore really beautiful. Across his torso he sports a red flannel bandolier. He wears a kilt

yuwsi'ytangwu. Pam oovi pay put
leenat piw yawtangwu.

Pam pi pay powamuytsöqa'a-
si'ytangwuniiqe oovi piw Popwa-
muytuy amun sihut nakwa'ytangwu.
Pam pi lensiningwu. Pay naalöyöm
angqw oomiq iitsiwyungwa, qötö-
veq. Pam pi pay tutskwava himu
sihu, uuyi lomahinyungniqat oovi
pam put tu'awi'yta. Pam piw ngölöshoya'ytangwu. Pay pam niikyangw
qa put aw naatöngtangwu. Pam pay
put yawtangwu. Pam pay ngölöshoya tsavawyangwu. Niikyangw
pam sakwawsaningwu. Piw it taawat
iikwiwtangwu. Pam Taawakopö pi
pay Soyohömkatsinmuy amumum
pitungwu. Katsinmuy su'amun
wunimangwu.

over which an embroidered kachina
sash and a Hopi belt are worn. The
attractive moccasins are bordered
with anklebands of colored designs.
In addition, the kachina carries a
flute.

Since his body is painted like
that of a Powamuy kachina, he sports
a flower on his head just like the ini-
tiates of the Powamuy society. That's
the so-called flute flower. Actually,
there are four of them on top of his
head, sticking up. They signify that
the flowers and plants across the land
are going to be beautiful. And also,
Taawakopö has a cane. But he does
not lean on it. He only carries it. It is
quite short and painted blue-green.
On his back he wears the sun
[shield]. As a rule, Taawakopö comes
with a group of Mixed kachinas and
dances just like them.

Kokopölmana, the Robber Fly Girl Kachina

Kokopölmana's Appearance and Behavior

Kookopölö's erotic counterpart is Kokopölmana, "Robber Fly Girl." Waters's (1963: 343) rendition of the name as "Humpback Locust Woman" is false on semantic as well as cultural grounds. In addition to creating confusion by identifying the insect *kookopölö*, "robber fly," as a locust, he translates the element *-mana* as "woman." The correct Hopi term for "woman" is *wuuti*, which occurs in such kachina names as Hahay'iwuuti and So'yokwuuti. The kachina name Kokopölmana consists of Kokopöl-, the regular combining form of Kookopölö, and *-mana*, the vowel-shortened combining form of *maana*, "girl, unmarried woman." *Maana* does not mean "wife" (Grant 1967: 60) or "sister" (Titiev 1939: 91 n. 4). The term simply means "girl," implying here that the sex and fertility aspects symbolically expressed in Kookopölö are also embodied in the female. Wellmann (1970: 1681) appropriately calls Kokopölmana Kookopölö's "companion in spirit." Text 35 describes the appearance of the goddess. Note that while this text concurs with Colton's (1970: 36) observation that Kokopölmana comes barefoot, his claim that she is equipped with a hump just like her male companion is ethnographically not corroborated.

Text 35

Kokopölmana pi pay put mit taaqat Kookopölöt pi pay antangwu. Pu' pay piw su'an as qötövaqe tuuwuhiwkyangw pam pay qa naqvu'ytangwu. Pam naasomtangwu. Pay pöhöt nasmi'ytangwu. Pam pankyangw pay as pi piw put taaqat su'an pe'ytangwu. Pu' pay kwasa'ytangwu, atö'hoyat torikiwtangwu. Pay pi ephaqam pi pay saskwit kwasa'ytangwu. Pu' ephaqam pi pay naat nukngwat ang pakiwtangwu.

Kokopölmana looks like the male Kookopölö. However, while she also has the white stripe over her head, she lacks ears. Instead, she has wool tied to the sides of her head in the typical *naasomi* hair style of unmarried women. Otherwise her mask is decorated like that of her companion. She wears the black woolen dress and has slung the *atö'ö* cape over one shoulder and under the other. Once in a great while, she wears a really

Kokopölmana qa pööla'yta; pay Kookopölösa'. Niikyangw pam pay ngasta tootsi'ytangwu, sukukvuyaw-tangwu. Kokopölmana pay qa hiita yaawi'yta, pam tootimuy, tataqtuy ngöynumngwuniiqe oovi. Pu' pam pay piw tuwat somivikit, tsukuvikit, tangu'vikit, pay puuvut hiita pam na'mangwu'ytangwu. Pu' pam tuwat pay oovi taaqat aqw yomimiykye' pu' paasat pay piw put aw sisvi-ngwu, put tsukuvikit, pu' pay tangu'-vikit, pay puuvut. Pam tuwat hapi Hopinösiwqa. Pam put siivuwta-ngwu, kwasay atpikyaqe piihuy anga.

tattered dress. Then again, she is garbed in something nice. Kokopölmana has no hump; only Kookopölö has this. She wears no shoes and is barefoot.

Kokopölmana also carries noth-ing in her hands when she chases the boys and men. Her gifts usually con-sist of *somiviki, tsukuviki, tangu'viki*, and other such foods. Each time she thrusts her hips into a man, she pays him in return with these dishes. They are made according to traditional Hopi recipes and are usually tucked away under her dress in the bust.

Like Kookopölö, Kokopölmana appears in the company of other kachinas. Titiev (1939: 94) reports that Kokopölmanas jointly perform with their male counterparts in the spring. At the occasion, the kachina impersonators "spend the forenoon gathering wild blossoms" that the Kookopölös then use in the afternoon to run *ngöytiw*, the "chasing game," with the Kokopölmanas who accompany them. This joint performance is extinct today. Nowadays, the Kokopölmana usually appears during *qöqöntinumya*, "the Powamuy kachina parade." Overall, it can be said that in her public display of sexual behavior she is much more aggressive than Kookopölö.

Text 36

Kokopölmana sutsep pi pay Powa-muyve qöqöntinumyaqw yamak-ngwuniqw hakim itsivu'iwyung-ngwu. Pam pi pay yamakye' pu' tootimuy tuwat amumi nuvö'iwte'

Whenever there is a kachina proces-sion during the Powamuy ceremony, the Kokopölmana also comes out. People are angry about that, for she is lusting after the young men and pumuy ngöynumngwu. Pu' tootim oovi apyeve waytinumyangwu. Pu' pam hiitawat ngu'e' angqe' munukne' pu' pay atsmi wupngwu. Pu' aqw yomimiykungwu. Pu' mimawat kyamat awye' pu' put ayo' tuuvayangwu, tiyot, taaqat kyamat. Pu' pam somivikiy pay amumi sisvingwu. Pam put somivikiy siivuwtangwu. Kokopölmana paay naap hisat pitungwu. Pay katsinmuy amumum piw wunimanik pitungwu, Wawarkatsinmuy amumum.

Pay hisathaqam yaw haqamwat kitsokive ima Kokopölmamant tiiva. Niiqe pay kiisonmiye' somivikiy siivuwyungngwu. Pu' pay tootimuy, taataqtuy amuupa yottiwisngwu. Pu' pay hiitawat ngu'e' pu' pay songqa aqw yomimiykungwu. Pu' aw somivikiy sisvingwu. Pas yaw ep tootim, taataqt qa kwangwatitimayya. Noq pay puma pan aasakis kiisonmiye' tiivanik pu' tootimuy, taataqtuy amuupa yottiwisngwu. Pay puma Wawarkatsinmuy su'amun tiiva.

chases them. So the boys run away from her. As she grabs hold of one, she trips him up so that he falls to the ground. Then she mounts him and thrusts her hips into him. The boy's aunts then run to his side and throw her off.[1] In return, Kokopölmana pays her victim with *somiviki*. That she carries tucked under her dress.

Kokopölmana will come at any time. If she really wants to dance, she usually comes with Runner kachinas.

Once the Kokopölmanas were performing a day dance at a certain village. Each time they came to the plaza, they had their *somiviki* tucked under their dresses in the bust. Then they went along holding it out among the boys and men. Whenever one of the Kokopölmanas grabbed one of them, she would thrust her hips into him. In return for this act she paid him with her *somiviki*. That day the boys and men did not have a good time watching the dance. Each time the Kokopölmanas returned to the plaza to dance, they held out their gifts among the menfolks. They danced just like the Runner kachinas.

---

1. Titiev (1938: 41) confirms this custom of intervening on behalf of the male who is being "raped" by the Kokopölmana: "The victim's paternal aunts are expected to rush to the defence of their beloved nephew and to tear him away from the embraces of this lascivious katcina."

Figure 6: Fluteplayers from south of Black Mesa
A rock art site located in an area south of Black Mesa in northeastern Arizona contains what may be the largest single concentration of prehistoric fluteplayer images. Totaling more than 175 figures, the sheer numbers as well as the wide variation in morphology, attributes, associations, and elaboration suggest that the symbol's origin may be traceable to this locale. Representing the major early development of the fluteplayer image, the symbol and its associated cultural features and traditions may have diffused throughout the Southwest from there. Fluteplayers in this region are only rarely depicted as humpbacked (g) and/or ithyphallic, and groupings of multiple figures are quite common (a, b, c, d, e, f, g, j).

Titiev (1939: 97) provides a rather vivid description of Kokopölmana's sexually aggressive behavior. Impersonated by a male, as is practically every kachina, she deals with her male victim in almost rapelike fashion.

As soon as this impersonator emerged from the kiva, all the men and boys in the vicinity began to scatter. At first the Kokopölmana merely feinted running after them, but suddenly "she" caught up with an unwary man, raised him high in "her" arms and pretended to copulate with him from behind. This done, "she" released him and handed him a few packets of somiviki (cornmeal cakes). From then on "she" ran far and wide in quest of "lovers," pretended to lure men out of their houses, and argued in vigorous pantomime with all women and girls who tried to keep men away from "her." In one instance Kokopölmana climbed to a roof top where a solitary man was intent on watching the other katcinas in the plaza below. "She" seized him without warning, threw him roughly to the ground and squeezed him in a tight embrace. A few moments later he was released, slightly dazed, and proffered the usual gift of somiviki.

Kokopölmana's appearance always creates a great stir among the male spectators, both married and unmarried. In addition to the embarrassment of the victim with whom she imitates intercourse—always to the great hilarity of the audience—there seems to be a Hopi belief that a man is "'spoiled' (that is, rendered undesirable to other girls) if the Kokopölmana 'gets into him'" (Titiev 1939: 98). Wright (1977: 76) similarly reports that according to the Hopi "a man is no good to his girl for a year after he has been caught" by the goddess.

As Text 37 points out, Kokopölmana also sexually taunts the women. She does so by exposing her thigh, a part of the female anatomy that, in the eyes of the Hopi male, is highly eroticizing. In this respect, the illustration of the goddess in Wright (1973: 231) is culturally accurate. Totally false, on the other hand, is the carved *tihu* in Erickson (1977: 103), where Kokopölmana exposes one of her breasts. A woman's breast is never mentioned as erotically attractive in Hopi culture. "Hollywoodized" carvings of this kind are acculturated products designed solely to appeal to the prurient taste of white kachina doll collectors. As Erickson (1978: 103) himself explains, such graphic depiction of the sexual anatomy in a kachina doll was part of a "pornographic fad" geared for the white collector's market.

Text 37

Pu' haqam wuutiniqw pu' aw tutu-tsiwe' qaasiy aw hölökni'ykyangw aw palalatoynangwu. Pay pi sen pi hakiy aapeniiqe qötsaqaasi'yta sen wukoqaasi'yta. Pam kya pi momoy-muy itsivulawngwuniiqe pu' pumuy taataqtuy pi pay amungk nuvö'iw-numngwu, tuungöylawngwu.

Pu' hakimuy mööyiyamuy taq'ayayamuy ngu'aqw pu' kyamat, tumsimat pu' pay kyaakyawnaya-ngwuniiqe oovi aw yuutukye' pu' ang ayo' Kokopölmanat tuuvaya-ngwu.

When there is a woman somewhere, Kokopölmana may make fun of her by exposing her thigh to the woman and slapping it quickly with her hand. Maybe to indicate that her thighs are more lightly complected and bigger. She typically manages to get the women angry and displays her desire for sex by chasing after the men.

When she grabs someone's grandson or other male clan member, the aunts and female clan relatives get jealous of her, and then they rush up to the kachina and throw her off her victim.

In addition to appearing in a group of Mixed kachinas, Kokopölmana also comes in the company of Wawarkatsinam, "Runner kachinas." As Wright (1973: 231) points out, at this occasion "she will induce someone to run against 'her' and then hoist her skirts and overtake him." By diverting her opponent's attention in this way, she usually wins the race, whereupon she will fling her hapless victim to the ground and give "a rough and graphic imitation of sexual intercourse" (Titiev 1938: 41). Texts 38 and 39 illustrate some of these details.

Text 38

Hisat pi pay piw Wawarkatsinam ökingwuniqw pay pam Kokopölma-

Long ago when Runner kachinas used to arrive to perform, Kokopöl

na pumuy amumum piw pitungwu.
Niikyangw pam pi pay tuwat taataqtuy wawarnangwu. Pay hiitawat wii-
kye' pu' angqe' tatskwekne' atsmiq
sutskikngwu. Pu' aqw yomimiykungwu.

Text 39

Pay pi Kokopölmana as piw pi qa
wawarkatsinaniqw pi pay pam
niikyangw pumuy amumum sutsep
pitungwu. Kya pam piw paniqw pay
hiitawat söwtoynaniqey oovi piw
pam amumumningwu. Pay warik-
niqw pay ngu'e' pay piw pan atsmi
wupngwu, angqe' tuuve'. Pay pam
oovi pumuy antsa amumum pitungwu, Wawarkatsinmuy amumum.
    Kokopölmana nuutuupa yomi-
mitinumngwu, pay kya pi pam
nuvöniiqe oovi. Pam pi pay qa hisat
wunima.
    Pam pay pumuy amumum piw
pitungwu. Wawarkatsinmuy amumumnen pu' pay pam hiitawat
wariknaqw amum warikqw pu' pam
put pay piw ngu'angwu. Ispi kwasa'at wuupaniqw pam kur hin warik-
ninik pu' pay hihin kwasay oomi
hölölangwu.

mana was normally one of them. She
too would challenge a man to race
with her. Whenever she caught up
with one, she would throw him on
the ground and quickly mount him.
Then she made pelvic thrusts into
him.

Kokopölmana is not a Runner kachina, but she often accompanies these
kachinas. Apparently, she comes in
order to slow down a runner. If one
is about to dash off, she may grab
him, only to mount him after flinging
him down. Therefore, she truly
comes with the Runner kachinas.
    Kokopölmana always goes
around making quick pelvic thrusts
into the menfolk, for she is horny and
thinking about sex. As a rule, she
never dances [in a dance formation
with a group of Kokopölmanas].
    She will come with the Runner
kachinas. As soon as she gets someone to run and races with him, she
catches him. Since her dress is long
and she cannot run well with it, she
always raises it up somewhat.

    Contrary to Wellmann's contention (1974: 2), the ritualistic copulation
carried out by Kokopölmana has not been "proscribed by the authorities." At

least, I have been able to witness repeated acts of simulated sex carried out by Kokopölmanas and Hopi spectators in the last decade. Nor can Kokopölmana's behavior be likened to that of "rasende Mänaden," that is, "orgiastic or frenzied maenads," as Hunger (1977: 700) postulates. A touch of lewdness, however, is detectable in a song dedicated to her. According to Emory Sekaquaptewa (1995, personal communication), the epithet *sivulöwamana*, "soot vagina girl," that is bestowed on Kokopölmana in this song "refers to the dark skin texture around the vagina and is a derogatory term."

Text 40

Kokopölmana, Kokopölmana.
Sivulöwmana, sivulöwmana.
Puma yang kaway'uyit, melon'uyit
Siitalawvaqö'ö puyayatangwu.
Sivulöwmana, sivulöwmana.

Kokopölmana, Kokopölmana.
Soot vagina girl, soot vagina girl.
Here over the watermelon plants,
the muskmelon plants they fly
when their flowers start blooming.
Soot vagina girl, soot vagina girl.

Kokopölmana and Fertility

Kokopölmana's ultimate purpose, however, is to assure the increase of the Hopi population, guaranteeing the survival of the group. Outwardly her copulatory antics may be hilarious and provide comic relief; this does not, however, as Hill (1995: 23) suggests, portray "the absurdity and humor of sexuality." Rather, it represents sympathetic increase magic, a point that is made again and again in the subsequent texts.

Text 41

Kokopölmana hapi sinot oovi pitungwu. Sinot wuuhaqtiniqat tuutsop-
tinumngwu. Pay hak oovi hakiy aw
pituqw qa waayangwu. Yan tutaplal-
wa. Noq pay piw watqangwu.

Kokopölmana comes because of the
people. She has intercourse with
them so that the population can increase. You must therefore not run
away from her when she approaches
you. That's how they instruct us. But
people run away anyway.

Text 42

I' Kokopölmana pi tuwat pay as pi
Kookopölöt ankyangw pam pi maa-
naniiqe oovi kwasa'yta. Pu' pam
tuwat imuy tootimuy, taataqtuy
ngöynumngwu. Navotiniqw yaw
pam imuy tootimuy naat puhuwu-
ngwiwyungqamuy pumuy pas
tuwatniqe oovi pumuy pas ngöynumngwu. Yaw pam pumuy tuwat
tootimuy kongtaniqe oovi yaw
pumuy pukumnaniqe ooviniqw
Hopit aw wuuhaqtiniqw paniqw
oovi pam pumuy tootimuy ngöynumngwu. Nen pu' himuwat ngu'e',
tuuve', pu' atsmiq wuuve' pu' aqw
yomimitangwu.
     Yan it piw Hopiit navoti'y-
yungqw oovi hakiy Kokopölmana
ngöyve' tuuvaqw pay hak nawus qa
aw rohomtingwu. Pay pam nawus
hakiy tsopngwu. Yan it piw Hopiit
navoti'yyungqw pu' pam hakiy
tsoove' pu' hakiy aw sisvingwu. Pam
sutsep it somivikit kinumngwuniiqe
pu' hakiy put aw pan sisvingwu. Pan
pam tuwat hintsakmaqe pu' pam
nuutumi noovat sisvingwu, hakiy
tsoove'.

The Kokopölmana is much like Kookopölö, but since she is a female, she
wears a dress. In addition, she is
always in pursuit of married and unmarried men. According to tradition,
she's especially chasing adolescent
boys. People say she wants to mate
with them so that she can deflower
them. She wants to see the Hopi population increase. That's the reason for
going after those boys. And when she
catches one, she flings him to the
ground, and then she mounts him
and thrusts her hips into him several
times.
     This is how the Hopis under-
stand this custom. Therefore, someone who is pursued by the Kokopölmana and thrown down must not
resist her. She has to have intercourse
with him. According to Hopi tradition Kokopölmana then pays whoever she had intercourse with. She
always carries *somiviki* [cornmeal
cakes] around with her that she uses
as payment. This is how the female
kachina carries on.

Text 43

Kokopölmana pi pay piw pitungwu-
niikyangw pam tuwat taataqtuy
amuupa yomimitinumngwu. Pay
piw pan hiitawat tsöpaate' tso'o'oy-
kinangwu, taaqat. Pay yaw pam
Kokopölmana yaw pay neengem
okiw piw tihut wuuhaqtiniqat
naawaknangwuniiqe oovi paniqw
pam taaqat tuwat aw pantingwu.

The Kokopölmana also appears. She
typically goes around among the
menfolk thrusting her hips into them.
She may even lift a man up and,
pressing him to her body, make him
jump up and down. People say
Kokopölmana wishes her children to
get plentiful. That's the reason she
treats a man in this manner.

Maahu, the Cicada

The Cicada-Locust Confusion

Of all the insects that are culturally significant to the Hopi people, the cicada is probably second only to the spider (in the person of Old Spider Woman) in importance. Known in all Hopi dialects as *maahu*, the term is linguistically part of a limited class of nouns that feature the absolutive suffix *-hu*. Hopi nouns of this type generally lose their absolutive ending in the process of pluralization or compounding. Thus, the correct plural form of *maahu* is *maatu*, not *mamaat* as is implied by Voth's misspelled form *mámahtu* (1905: 218). The occurring combining forms are vowel-shortened *ma-* as in *maktuki*, "parched cicadas," and *maa-* as in Maatikive, "Cicada kachina dance." However, the full forms *mahu-* and *-mahu* with a shortened first syllable are also attested. The former occurs in *mahulakvu*, "molted cicada shell," and the diminutive *mahuwya*, "little cicada"; the latter appears in *tumamahu*, "kaolin-colored cicada," possibly a reference to the newly-emerged adult cicada that initially is "pale or white, but gradually turns brown" (Capinera 1995: 84).

From all indications, the mistranslation of *maahu* as "locust," so pervasive in the ethnographic literature (mirroring the widespread usage of "locust" for "cicada" in the general population), was already well established in the early days of Hopi-Anglo contact. Cushing (1923: 167), in an origin myth that he recorded during his visit to the Third Mesa village of Oraibi in 1883, employs the term "locust." However, the myth, which was published posthumously by Parsons, did not become available to the general public until 1923. Stephen too uses the semantic equation "*maahu*, 'locust,'" in a narrative that he collected in 1893 on First Mesa (his "Hopi Tales" were not published, however, until 1929). Voth, the famous missionary who seems to have dedicated more of his time at Oraibi to the recording of Hopi secular and ceremonial life than to proselytizing Hopis to the Mennonite faith, was the first to propagate the misnomer in writing (1905: 217–20).

As Capinera (1995: 84) points out, "in virtually all anthropological accounts, cicada is called locust. However, *locust* is an old-world term applied to grasshoppers that tend to aggregate into swarms and migrate, forming damaging plagues." It is highly unlikely that the Hopi would have attributed so many positive associations to the harmful locust as, indeed, they did to the harmless cicada. Nor is there, to my knowledge, any evidence that the Hopi ever suffered crop loss or damage owing to traveling swarms of locusts. The widespread use of "locust" for "cicada" apparently owes its origin to European settlers who brought the term to America without seriously questioning the entomological reality of the insect (Peter Price, personal communication). Beaglehole (1937: 35) was the first to correctly identify the Hopi *maahu* as a cicada. Still, his observation did not help to eradicate the semantic misalignment of the insect with the locust, for it continues with great tenacity in all published ethnographic and anthropological accounts.

This semantic distinction is important because cicadas have, as do some rock art fluteplayers, what can appear to be a hump, whereas locusts do not. Entomologically, cicadas, also known as harvest flies, belong to the large superfamily Homoptera. Literally denoting "same [pairs of front and back] wings," the superfamily is distinguished by "membranous-winged bugs that subsist on vegetarian tissue" (Klausnitzer 1987: 98). Ranked "among the largest of plant-sucking insects" (O'Toole and Preston-Mafham 1985: 23), "cicadas are medium to large in size, and easily recognized by the wide blunt head with prominent eyes and the long, clear membranous forewings which are held peaked over the body at rest. They have three distinct ocelli, short bristle-like antennae, plainly visible proboscis, stout front legs, and three-jointed tarsi" (Swan and Papp 1972: 132). Capinera (1995: 84), an entomologist, points out that the insect's "general humpbacked appearance caused by the enlarged prothorax, so evident in the nymph, is only slightly diminished in the adult." Text 44 represents a less sophisticated description of the insect by a Hopi consultant.

Text 44

Maahu pi pay momot anhaqam soniwngwuniikyangw pam qa pantangwu. Pam pay pas wuuyaqat, wuupat masa'ytangwu. Pam pay qa momot an sikyangput puukya'ytangwu.	A cicada looks somewhat like a bee. It has long and broad wings. But its skin is not yellow like that of a bee. Rather it is gray. The insect gives a grayish impression.

Pam pay pas maasi, pay hihin masi-
hintangwu.

Cicadas as Food

From all evidence, the Hopis long ago developed a culinary fancy to the cicada and used the insect during the summer months to supplement their dietary
needs. Thus, the entire plot of "The Crying Cicada" rests on the custom of the
people of Oraibi to treat the insect as a culinary item. This use of cicadas as
food is reported in Voth (1905: 181–82); the mini-tale in Text 45 alludes to the
same ethnographic fact.

Text 45

Aliksa'i. Yaw kur yang aasupoq yee-
siwa, Songoopave, Orayve, Supawla-
ve, Musangnuve, Walpe, Sitsom'ove,
Hanokive. Noq Hopiit maahut kwa-
ngwa'yyungwa. Yaw pumuy tutskwava maqnumya. Noq haqam
suwaptsoki yawi. Noq ooveq tsokiw-
ta maahu. Noq yaw hak tiyooya ngu-
'aniqe aw wayma. Yan tawlawu pam
maahu:

> Maahu, maahu,
> Maahu, maahu.
> Leelena, Leelena,
> Leelena, leelena.
> Suwaptsokit ooveq
> tsokiwkyangw
> Leelena, leelena.
> Aapiy höngiwmakyangw.
> Ruk.

Paasat pam waaya. Waayaqw pam
tiyo kyawna. "Aya," yaw kita.

Aliksa'i. People were living all over
the land here, at Shungopavi, Oraibi,
Shipaulovi, Mishongnovi, Walpi, and
Hano. Hopis really like to eat cicadas,
so they go hunting for them here on
the land. There was some sagebrush
somewhere, and on it sat a cicada. A
boy, anxious to catch it, moved up to
it. This is how the cicada sang:

> Cicada, cicada,
> Cicada, Cicada.
> Is fluting, is fluting,
> Is fluting, is fluting.
> Sitting on a sagebrush
> It is fluting, fluting.
> Quickly it was gone.
> Ruk.

After it flew off, the boy felt sorry for
having lost it. "Too bad," he cried.

That the consumption of cicadas is not a figment of Hopi oral tradition is obvious in Text 46, a detailed recipe for the preparation of *maktuki*, "parched cicadas." One of my consultants still remembers having been offered side-dishes of fried cicadas in the Third Mesa village of Hotevilla in pre–World War II days. Today, the custom of eating cicadas is no longer practiced.

Text 46

Pumuy maatuy pi pay hak kutukta-nik pumuy oovi maqtongwu. Pu' wuuhaq pumuy haqe'nen pu' pumuy tsamve' pu' naksivuy tsokyangwu. Pantit pu' atpipoq qööngwu. Pu' angqw naakit ayo' paas tsamngwu. Nen pu' wihut angqw tsöqe' pu' put aqw panangwu. Pu' pam pavan mu-kiitiqw pu' maatuy aqw siwukna-ngwu. Pu' tutsayat wuuyaqat tavi'y-te' pu' put aqw su'uutangwu. Pantit pu' atpikyaqe aqw qöritangwu. Pu' puma hihin kwasiye' kwangwako-lakngwu. Paasat pu' pumuy angqw tsamngwu ahoy. Pu' öngaspalkukye' pu' pumuy aqw mortoynayakyangw piikiy enang noonovangwu.

If a woman wants to parch cicadas, she must first go hunt for them. Upon getting a lot and returning with them, she puts the kettle that is nor-mally used for parching corn on the fire. She lights a fire under it and after removing any sand left in the vessel she takes some pinches of fat and puts them inside. Once the fat is really hot, the cicadas are poured in. Then she takes a large sifter and closes off the top of the kettle. Hav-ing done that she stirs the insects. They are done as soon as they turn a nice, crispy brown. At that point, they are removed from the vessel. People now make a salt brine into which they dip the cicadas while eating them together with *piki*.

The Cicada and the Flute

Best known for their loud buzzing and whistling sounds, produced exclusive-ly by males as an acoustic ploy to attract females, cicadas have caught the attention of humankind in cultures around the globe (Klausnitzer 1987: 98–99). Responsible for the loud trilling sound is "a pair of vibrating organs called timbals that are located in the abdomen" (Knauth 1970: 96). To the Hopi ear the sound of the singing insect is reminiscent of that emanating from a *leena*, "flute," the Hopis' only wind instrument. For this reason a cicada is believed to be the owner of a flute. *Leelena*, "to be fluting," the reduplicated form of *leena*, is therefore used to describe the cicada's sounds linguistically. To be sure, the distinct proboscis of the insect may have reinforced this cultural association with the wind instrument, for as Capinera (1995: 85) observes, "when examined from below, the long tubular mouthparts of the cicada extend from the base of the head down between the legs. A dead cicada or nymphal exuvium truly appears to be playing an end-blown flute." Text 47 explains this phenomenon from a Hopi point of view.

Text 47

Pam pi pay qa hiita leenat yawta-ngwuniikyangw pam pay pan töötö-ki'ytangwu. Pam pay naap put tö-na'yta. Pam tuwat leelenngwu. Pay pas piw kwangwalelenngwu. Pam pay oovi qa hiita leenat ang as leelen-ngwuniikyangw pam pay pas put pantaqat kya pi motsovu'ytaqe oovi. Pam oovi pay pang leelenngwu, put anga'.

The cicada does not carry a flute, but that's what it sounds like when it sings. It has its own voice, which is fluting. The insect does that very melodiously. While it has no flute, I guess it has a snout resembling one. Through that it flutes.

Cicadas, Heat, and the Len Society

From the viewpoint of entomology, the cicada's "frequency of sound production is directly related to temperature. Adults are especially vocal on hot days" (Capinera 1995: 84). In the eyes of the Hopi, this causal relationship works exactly the other way around: It is the insect's music that is held responsible for hot weather. For this reason, Waters (1963: 37), although mistranslating *maahu* as "locust," correctly characterizes it as the "insect which has the heat power." Text 48 explains this in conjunction with *tööngi*, "hot weather, heat of the day."

Text 48

Maahu tööngit himu'yta; oovi lee-lenqw kwangqattingwu.

The cicada has the heat; so the weather gets warm when the insect flutes.

Beaglehole's comment (1937: 35) that "to hear many cicadas singing in the trees means a hot summer and little rain" carries a negative implication in that it seems to conjure up the prospect of drought triggered by the insect's command over heat. Nothing could be further from the truth. Hot weather induced by the music of the cicada is considered desirable and highly beneficial by the Hopis. They believe that warm temperatures promote growth and maturation of crops, as is evident from Text 49.

Text 49

Pay pi pam tuwat yang uuyit ang yaw waynume' pay leelenngwu. Uuyit pumuy öqalannumngwu. Pam mukit tuwi'yta.	The cicada roams the corn plants playing its flute. It goes around encouraging them, for it owns the heat.

This important conceptual association of the cicada with heat and the fecundating season is also corroborated in the context of Hopi oral literature. For example, in "The Cicadas and the Serpents," which takes place in mythtime when humans and animals still had the capability of assuming each other's shapes, a cicada, at one point, picks up his flute and, using it like a flame-thrower, clears a path through the snow for his serpent visitor.

In "The Crying Cicadas," the insects depart from Hopiland in disgust because they are tired of being hunted down to satisfy dietary needs. As a result, the weather turns cold, the land does not warm up in summer any longer, and the crops are late in maturing.

In "The Boy Who Went in Search of the Cicadas," the hero actually sets out looking for the source of the heat power. After many tests he encounters Cicada and learns that the insects left the Hopis because they felt ceremonially neglected by them. To remedy the situation and guarantee their growth-promoting singing, the Hopis will henceforth be expected to fashion *pahos*, "prayer-sticks," for the insect population.

That the Hopis indeed appealed to the cicada by means of special prayer items is borne out in Text 50.

Text 50

Pay ima hisat wimwiwimkyam imuy maatuy maqnumyangwu. Pu' himuwa pumuy sakine' hiisa' qöye' pu' kohot ang hotomnangwu. Pantaqat pay tavi'ytangwu. Pu' hisat puma paaholalwaniqw piw pu' himuwa maatuy hotomni'ytaqey put enang yawmangwu, kivamiq. Pu' enang paahotangwu. Noq pu' yaw kwang-qattingwu.

In the old days the initiated members of religious societies used to hunt for cicadas. Whenever one of them lucked out and killed a few, he would pierce them on a little stick and store them in this way. At the time prayer sticks were made the one who had the pierced cicadas would bring them to the kiva. There prayer sticks were fashioned with them. As a result, the weather usually turned nice and warm.

Pahos of this kind were usually prepared during Soyalangw, the "Soyal or Winter Solstice ceremony," which was celebrated in the Hopi month of Kyaamuya, approximately December. Text 51 alludes to this custom.

Text 51

Pu' oovi himuwa pay pumuy hiisa'niiqamuy tal'angwnawit maskyate' pu' pam pumuy enang paahotangwu. Pay sen oovi Soyalangwuy angqe'.

Some people put some cicadas aside during the summer months and use them later when they make prayer sticks, which is probably around the time of the Soyal ceremony.

Although Text 50 is not specific in regard to which religious organizations used cicadas for some of their prayer sticks, all ethnographic data point to the two Hopi Len societies, the Masilelent, "Gray Flutes," and the Sakwalelent, "Blue Flutes." As a rule, however, Hopis do not bother to differentiate the two fraternities; instead, they simply refer to them as Leelent, "Flutes." Members of these Len societies regard the cicada as their *pooko*, as illustrated in Text 52. Literally meaning "pet," *pooko* is often best rendered as "patron" or "totem."

Text 52

Pay ima Leelent it maahut pooko'y- yungngwu. Pu' puma leelenyanik, pavasiwyanik pu' put maahuy, poo- koy, saaqat oomiq tsokyayangwu. Pu' pam tuwat pepeqwat leelen- ngwu.	The Len society members have the cicada as a totem. Whenever they intend to play their flutes and engage in ritual prayer, they put their totem on top of the [kiva] ladder, where it flutes for them.

The significance that is accorded the cicada's heat power has already been seen in Hopi emergence mythology. After exiting from the underworld at Sipaapuni, the various Hopi clans set out on their migrations. The Flute clan, which had the cicada as its *wu'ya,* "clan totem," employed the magic heat powers of the insect. When the group encountered a massive barrier of ice and snow in the north, as is related in Text 53, the insect proved powerless and failed to melt the obstacle. In spite of this intimate relationship between the Flute clan and the cicada, the insect apparently never served the clan as a clan emblem. Turner's (1963: 25) contention that "the humped-back flute player … during the 10th and 11th centuries when he makes his first appearance in the Glen Canyon region … must have represented … [among other things] a clan symbol," is refuted by Hopi rock art itself. At Tutuventiwngwu, the "Clan Rock" site near Willow Springs, famous for its hundreds of Hopi clan symbols that were engraved there over the centuries by salt-faring Hopis on the way to the Grand Canyon, not a single fluteplayer icon can be found. And yet, many members of the Flute clan must have embarked on this journey in the past.

Text 53

Ima pi Lenngyam nankwusaqe puma put pooko'ywisa. Pam pumuy wu'- ya'amniqw pu' oovi puma kwi- niwiqhaqami, nuvasonmiq öki. Pepehaq ökiiqe pu' pas yaw sutsep a'ni nuva'iwtaqw puma put qa angwu'ynumya. Pu' mi' maahu, pok'am, haktonsa yaw sutsep as	When the Flute Clan set out on its migration, its members took the cicada along as their pet. This insect is their clan ancestor. Finally they reached a place way in the northwest that was covered with snow. Since there was snow on the ground all the time, they failed to cope with it. The

leelena. Niikyangw yaw pam put kwingyawuy qa angwu'ynuma. Pam yaw nuwu okiw tuusung'iwta. Paas tuusungwtiqe paapu okiw hihin tsirtoyna. It pi pay yan yu'a'atota puma antsa Lenngyam pangsoq-haqamiyaqe pu' puma pay pangqw piw ahoyya.

cicada, their pet, kept playing its flute constantly, but to no avail. It could not overpower the cold northwest wind. Meanwhile, the cicada, poor thing, was shivering with cold. Eventually it was frozen to a point that it could only produce some chirping sounds. The Flute clan members claim that this truly happened. So, having arrived at that place they had to turn back again.

The specific link between the Len society and the insect is also confirmed in "The Boy Who Went in Search of the Cicadas." The cicadas in this legend actually charge the Len initiates to ceremonially care for them, not only during summer when they stage their public performance but also during their esoteric winter rites.

Ethnographically detailed descriptions of ceremonial Len activities at various Hopi villages, including pictorial renditions of Len altars, are found in the literature and shed some light on the function of the Len ritual (Fewkes 1894, 1895, and 1896; Voth 1912; Titiev 1944; Nequatewa 1946; Rosenberger 1956). Titiev (1944: 149) sees the most significant aspect of the Len ceremonies as "solar." This seems plausible considering the fact that immediately following the Soyal ceremony in December the task of the *taawat wiiki'ymaqa* (Malotki 1983a: 428), the Hopi term for the Anglo concept of "Sun Watcher," was entrusted to "the Gray Flute chief, whose duty it is to observe the sun's path until the summer solstice is reached" (Titiev 1944: 146). A symbolic reminder of this intimate connection between the Len society and the sun can readily be seen in the *taawa'ikwilni*, "sunshield," carried on the back of ceremonial participants as they attend to their rites at the village spring (Webb and Weinstein 1973: 107, plate 83).

Titiev's observation (1944: 149) that "Flute performances are invariably associated with warm weather, for the Hopi believe that the flutes represent the sounds of locusts [cicadas], who are regarded as harbingers of summer" additionally underlines the strong conceptual ties between the religious frater-

Figure 7: Middle Little Colorado River Valley fluteplayers

Fluteplayer images occur in small numbers at numerous individual sites scattered all along the middle Little Colorado River. As a rule, they consist of simple stick figures, occasionally ithyphallic (b, c, p) and rarely humpbacked (h, l, m). Some elaborations, including enlarged feet (i, l, m, q), horns or a headdress (b, c, p), variable flute configurations (a, g, m), and unusual fluteplayer postures (a, g, q) occur. Some figures may be early, based on their similarities to figures illustrated earlier (see Figure 6).

nity and the cicada. They are further corroborated by the portrayal of the flute-playing *maahu*, "cicada," on Len altar tiles (Stephen 1936: 790 and plate 22).

Bradfield (1973: 187) argues from the premise that the major observances of the two Len fraternities are held in August. By staging their culminating rites at the main spring of the village, they thereby "ensure the domestic water supply of the village at a time when, in the event of the failure of the summer rains, the flow of those springs has reached a critically low level."

Into this associative complex of ideas—cicada, flute, Len society, sun, heat, and germination—also fits an interesting rite that Voth has preserved (1905: 220). According to his narrator, "the locusts [cicadas] bring warm weather," which "is the reason why the priests often, when they make *pahos* in winter, throw pieces of a locust [cicada] on the fireplace and burn it because the smoke and odor bring warm weather." This explanation is given in the context of a narrative titled "The Snakes and the Locusts" (Voth 1905: 217–20), a variant version of "The Cicadas and the Serpents." At one point in the tale, Voth's narrator remarks that "The Locusts [cicadas] sometimes play flutes in a ceremony and that was the reason why it was so nice and warm there" (1905: 219). On the basis of the close association of cicadas and flutes one can assume, I believe, that the priests involved in the cicada-burning activity are Len priests carrying out an act of sympathetic magic.

Tyler (1975: 125), on the other hand, regards the Len ceremony primarily as "the major vegetation ritual of the Hopi." Evidence for this interpretation may be seen in the fact that the germination deity Muy'ingwa occurs as an integral part of the Mishongnovi (Fewkes 1896: plate 1) and Walpi (Stephen 1936: fig. 426) Len altars.

This emphasis on solar and vegetal fertility, however, must not obscure the fact that all Hopi ceremonies, including that of the Len, essentially constitute prayers for life-sustaining water. When the flutes are played by the Len members during their biennial public summer ceremony at the village spring, their ultimate purpose is to attract rain. While the rain association with the cicada is not foremost on a Hopi's mind, it is nevertheless attested in a short tale collected by Lockett (1933: 98–99). Titled "The Frog and the Locust [cicada]," the two creatures, at one point in the story, concur that the reason for their singing is "to make it rain" (Lockett 1933: 99).

The same equation of cicadas with members of the Len society is revealed in the final passages of "The Cicadas and the Serpents," when the narrator makes it clear that the cicadas "came transformed as human beings, just like us. Each one carried a flute."

According to Titiev (1944: 146 n. 26), the Sakwalen, or "Blue Flute," society at Oraibi was controlled by the Spider clan, whereas the Masilen, "Gray Flute," society was under the guidance of the Patki clan. This explains the intimate relationship of the Spider clan with the cicada, as may be gathered from Text 54.

Text 54

Ima Kookyangwngyam it maahut himu'yyungwa, wu'ya'yyungwa. Pu' piw it Leeniwuy enang himu'yyungwa. Niiqe oovi puma putakw sinmuy amungem naanawaknangwu. Iits mukipkinaqat oovi puma put maahut leelenniqat ayatotangwu. Noq oovi pam leelenqw pay iits mukipkingwu. Oovi kwangqatniqw pay puma yaktangwu.

The Spider clan people have the cicada as their clan ancestor. They also own the Flute society. So they pray by means of these for all people. They tell the cicada to flute so that the weather will turn warm soon. So, when the insect flutes, it gets hot early. This means that when the days are nice and warm, the cicadas are out and about.

Since the Spider clan considers Kookyangwso'wuuti, "Old Spider Woman," as their clan ancestor, she is frequently said to have the cicada as a pet. Once again, the cicada symbolizes the embodiment of magic heat power. In one episode that I recorded in conjunction with the legend of "The Destruction of Awat'ovi" (Malotki 1993: 323), the protagonist Pavayoykyasi, in a crop-growing contest with Lepenangwtiyo, "Icicle Boy," is aided by Old Spider Woman, *dea ex machina* extraordinaire in Hopi mythology. With the help of her pet cicada, she eventually breaks the cold spell caused by Lepenangwtiyo's icicles, instigates summerlike warmth, and induces magic growth and maturation of the sown crops.

The special relationship between the ancient earth goddess, the insect, and the Len ritual is summarized in the folk statement preserved in Text 55.

Text 55

Noq pu' i' Hopi piw pan navoti'y-taqw i' Kookyangwso'wuuti piw it maahut pooko'yta. Noq oovi qa iits kwangqattiqw pu' pam put horok-naqw pu' pam leelenqw paasat pu' piw kwangqattingwu. Noq oovi it Leeniwuy ep pam Kookyangwso'-wuuti piw put horoknangwu. Noq pam pi piw put wiimit himu'yta. Niiqe oovi yaw pumuy pangsoq pongyay aw yesvaqw paasat pu' yaw puma Leelent put maahut pangso iipo horoknaye' pu' puma put saaqat sus'oveq saqleetayat aw put tso-kyaqw pu' pam pep leelenlawqw paasat pu' yaw kwangqattingwu. Niiqe oovi hisat hakimuy piw amumi pangqaqwangwu, "Uma qa pumuy yuuyuynayamantani. Taq pay pu-muy amutsviy piw iits kwangqatti-ngwu," kitotangwu hakimuy amumi.

According to Hopi tradition Old Spider Woman has the cicada as a pet. So, when the weather does not get warm early in the season, she brings it out, and then it flutes. As a result, the days get nice and warm. The Len ceremony is another occa-sion when Old Spider Woman brings out the insect. For she also owns this ceremony. So, when the Flute ini-tiates have settled down by their altar, they take the cicada outside and place it on the topmost rung of the ladder. As the insect is fluting there, the weather turns nice and warm. Therefore, they used to warn us in the old days, "Don't pester these creatures. It's because of them that it gets hot early in the year."

Cicadas and Medicine Power

Various references in the literature assign medicinal and curative powers to the cicada. Parsons (1938: 338) insists that "Locust [cicada], the unwinking, is a brave man, a suitable patron for societies that cure for lightning shock and, inferably, for arrow and gun wounds." Essentially, this interpretation is derived from three episodes in the context of Hopi emergence myths in which the insect miraculously asserts its immortality. The fact that the cicada is part of several emergence and origin myths is a good indicator not only of its over-all significance in Hopi cosmology but probably also that the insect has been deeply entrenched in Hopi oral traditions for a long time.

As is to be expected in a situation where oral traditions are not fixed in print, there is no urtext of the emergence scenario against which the many narrative versions could be measured. Geertz (1984: 238) lists a dozen emergence narratives originating from Third Mesa alone. However, only two of these make reference to the cicada. In the Cushing version (1923: 163–70), recorded at the village of Oraibi in 1883 but not published until forty years later by Parsons, Locust, the familiar misnomer for Cicada, is commanded to return to the underworld because he is not considered "useful" by the people around him. Upon his refusal to obey, the people become so enraged that they kill the insect with their arrows. However, after Cicada comes back to life again, the people recognize his power of life-renewal as beneficent and decide that henceforth he shall "become the medicine of mortal wounds and war" (Cushing 1923: 168).

None of my Hopi consultants were able to recall any lore in which cicada medicine heals deadly injuries. Nevertheless, the indestructibility of the cicada is also echoed in Stephen's emergence version (1929: 3–6). As it turns out, Cicada here becomes the champion of the people desiring to leave the corrupt and chaotic underworld, for he is the first who succeeds in climbing the reed stalk and emerging into the new surface world. However, as he begins to play his flute, he provokes the wrath of the four Cloud deities, who resent the invasion of their territory. Yellow Cloud, chief of the north, first hurls his lightning bolt at the insect, but when the latter is not intimidated and plays on without batting an eyelid, the remaining three directional Cloud chiefs shoot their lightning missiles through him. Cicada, undaunted, survives this ultimate test and continues to flute as if nothing had happened. At this point, the four Cloud chiefs concede that he is "brave and deathless" (Stephen 1929: 6). They permit him not only to bring up his people, but they actually bestow their land on them. Cicada's behavior in this emergence episode bestows on him all the hallmarks of a culture hero. Russel (1991: 36), alluding to the same event, characterizes the flute-playing insect in somewhat overdramatic terms as "a Promethean figure who submits to painful tests so that mankind can live on earth."

This same theme of Cicada's unflinching courage and invulnerability occurs in the version presented by Waters (1963: 37–40). Geertz (1984: 238) severely criticizes Waters's emergence version and rejects it on the grounds that "it is synthetic, pan-Mesa retelling concocted by Waters, Oswald White Bear Fredericks and Otto Pentiwa." While I concur with his judgment, Waters's synchretistic pan-Hopi version nevertheless consists of individual narrative episodes that ring true. This also holds for the segment with the locust (cicada), much of which is presented in dialogue fashion, usually a hallmark of genuine folklore.

This time not one but two cicadas are tested by an eagle as the people, freshly emerged from their netherland homes, embark on their wandering across the continent. Once more the two cicadas, for which later "the Blue Flute and Gray Flute clans and societies were named" (Waters 1963: 38), neither blink when nearly poked into the eye by the eagle's arrow nor cease playing their flutes when transfixed with arrows. "The two *mahus* ... played their flutes still more tenderly and sweetly, producing a soothing vibration and an uplift of spirit which healed their pierced bodies" (Waters 1963: 37). As a result, the eagle gives them permission to occupy the land.

None of the emergence myths that I was able to record in the field, whether complete or in fragmentary form, from Third and Second Mesa consultants allude to the incredible fortitude and the fantastic healing powers of the cicada. The only instance in which one of my accounts refers to the insect happens in connection with the postemergence wanderings of the Spider clan.

Text 56

Ima Kookyangwngyam pu' put maahut pooko'yyungngwuniiqe oovi Kawestimay aqwwat nankwusaqe qa sakinaya. Iyoho' pepeqniqw qa taaviwvangwu. Pu' oovi puma put maahuy kivats'oveq taviyaqe pu' aw pangqaqwa, leelenniqat. Pu' taaviwvani. Pu' oovi pam pepeq ooveq tsokiwkyangw leelenngwu, naaqavo. Qa mukipkiqw nuwu pam maangu'i. Pu' as pam leelenlawngwu, nii-

The Spider Clan people, who have the cicada as their totem animal, started out toward Kawestima but were not very fortunate there. It was cold there and the sun would not shine. So they placed their cicada on the rooftop and told it to flute, hoping that then it would get sunny. The insect sat there on top fluting day in, day out. But the weather did not get warm. Meanwhile the cicada grew kyangw pay qa pas qa angwuta kwingyawuy. Paapu hihin tsirtoynaqw pu' put ahoy piw panaya. Pay kur son pam mukipkini, pepeq. Peep puma mahupkoy tusungninaya.

tired. It kept singing but failed to overpower the cold north wind. At one point it could only produce a few chirping sounds. It just was not going to get warm there. They almost killed their totem animal by freezing it to death.[1]

Cicada the Kachina

One last indicator, finally, for the veneration accorded the cicada in Hopi culture is the fact that it is one of five insects that achieved divine status as a kachina. The reason for the insect's deification can be gathered from Text 57. Note that the cicada is here said to be the proprietor of *mumkiw*, "the heat process" or "the process that warms the earth each year," rather than *tööngi*, as in Text 48, which merely alludes to "warm weather" and "heat of the day."

Text 57

Maahut katsintota, pay pi son pi qa kwangqatniqat oovi. Mumkiwuy himu'ytaqw oovi.

They obviously made the cicada into a kachina so that it can be nice and warm. After all, he is the owner of the warming process.

Known as Maahu, he is distinguished by an orange-colored mask that is topped by two horns symbolizing the insect's antennae. The kachina nowadays only appears during kiva night dances in the spring, as a rule in the company of Soyohömkatsinam, "Mixed kachinas." Titiev (1937: 256), in the context of a myth, reports the term Maatikive, "Locust [cicada] dance," an indication that in former times the insect was most certainly also performed in public plaza dances. None of my consultants was able to confirm the existence of such a dance. This is understandable because Titiev's narrator (1937: 256, n.

---

1. An episode similar to that recorded in Text 56 is also found in Geertz (1994: 350–51).

20) had no recollection of it at the time, other than that it was "an old-fashioned dance." For a detailed description of the kachina's mask see Colton (1970: 76); a full-color illustration of the kachina god is available in Wright (1973: 155).

The Cicada and Divinatory Power

To conclude this ethnographic portrait of the cicada in Hopi culture, a brief cicada reference is to be cited here that is somehow alien to the body of ideas associated with the insect. Parsons (1938: 338), almost in passing and without additional comment or reference to the source of the information, mentions that "the Flute Societies have locust [cicada] medicine to dream coming events, possibly in war." Ten years later, Renaud (1948: 40), repeats this statement in slightly more elaborate fashion. "The Flute Societies have a Locust [cicada] medicine, a potion or philter, which causes one to dream of things to come, and permits one to foresee future events especially, so it seems, in war."

None of my consultants were able to corroborate this notion of cicada medicine used for divinatory purposes. There is some evidence that Hopi medicine men used datura or jimsonweed to induce visions while making a diagnosis (Whiting 1966: 89). Titiev (1972: 54) reports of a Hopi doctor who gave one of his patients something to chew "that would cause him to dream and thus learn the identity of the witches who were after him." Unfortunately, the medicine that he administered is not identified, but it may also have involved datura. The highly poisonous and hallucinogenic plant was also widely used at Zuni for a variety of reasons, among others clairvoyance and divination. Stevenson (1915: 56) specifically relates that Zuni medicine men gave it to their clients so that they could discover the perpetrators of certain thefts. It is therefore possible that Parsons, who worked with a number of Puebloan cultures, got some of her ethnographic data confused and wrongly attributed dream- or vision-inducing properties to cicada medicine rather than datura. We will of course never know, so this last shred of information concerning the cicada will have to remain unverified.

Part 2

KOOKOPÖLÖ AND CICADA: SIX HOPI TALES

The Man-Crazed Woman

Aliksa'i. People were living at Qa'ötaqtipu. In addition, they were settled in the villages of Huk'ovi and Tiposqötö.

At Qa'ötaqtipu a boy from Huk'ovi had taken a wife. At first, the girl had not loved anyone. But she was very beautiful, and when she met this boy, she grew to like him, fell in love with him, and married him. Now the two were living there as husband and wife.

It so happened that this woman was man-crazed, and since her husband did not satisfy her at all, she disliked him and abused him. The mistreatment he received living with her was such that he finally became ill from it. As a result, the man began to sulk, and whenever he was in this mood, there was no telling what he would do. Usually, he wandered out to the mesa edge on the southeast and just sat there, his mind full of worries. He had no real desire to go on living with his wife any more. Every so often he felt like throwing himself down the cliffs on the southeast side. But then he would not have the courage to follow through, and would return to his wife's home again. His married life was one great misery.

Long ago people used to have races, and this man participated with the others in this kind of activity. He was an excellent runner, and whenever there was a kickball race, he came in first for his group, kicking the ball up to the mesa top. He also was an industrious farmer. He really had his heart in his fields. He worked hard in them and in return harvested large crops. That, however, did not impress his wife, for to a man-crazed woman such as she, running and farming meant nothing. The thing that mattered most to her was his kwasi, so her husband was nothing to her.

One day the man, who had been abused by his wife, was again sitting by the mesa edge, fraught with worries. As he sat there he kept thinking, "If I jump off here, I won't have to go home and suffer her mistreatment any more. She won't feel any sense of loss. Nor do I have relatives in my wife's village. Even in my own village I have no relatives." This is what went through his mind as he was sitting there. When evening came, the man finally overcame his inhibitions and was willing to go through with his suicide plan. As a result, he flung himself down. The cliff at this place was rather high, and it took a while until he struck the ground. The instant he did, he passed out and was not aware what had happened to him.

Some time later someone came along, talking as he approached the man. At this point the man came to again and opened his eyes. A stranger was sitting by his side and said to him, "Get up! Why are you doing this to yourself? You shouldn't have done such a foolish thing! How could you hurt yourself of your own free will? How could you wrong yourself in this way? You should have asked somebody for medicine. There is a medicine for your problem you know."

When the man heard the stranger talk like that, he recognized who it was. It was no other than Badger, who had his den nearby. From there he had observed the man as he sat by the precipice again and again. He knew what had been on his mind and had come over to him after he jumped down. Once again Badger spoke. "Rather than jumping off you could have asked for help. Someone would have prepared a medicine for you. You know, there's a remedy for this. It's stiffening medicine," he revealed to him. Then he continued, "No doubt, you broke your spine. Because of this injury you won't get well right away. I certainly can't help you with that. That's not within my power. But I do have this stiffening medicine. That I can give you. And I'll tell you how to use it," he said. "Anyway, you'll recuperate. After all, it wasn't your heart which got damaged. You won't die. Somehow you'll get well and manage to get back home. The stiffening medicine that I'll give you now you must take later. Once you take it, you can couple all you want. Just make sure you swallow the medicine before you're going to have sex. Then you'll always be able to hold a strong and stiff kwasi. You only need to bite off a little piece of the medicine. Also, before you swallow it, always rub a little of the juice together with some saliva on your hips." With that Badger handed him the erection remedy and trotted back home.

The man was in great pain. Obviously, something was injured. Badger had told him that his spine was broken. Hence, the man felt he had no choice but to stay there at the bottom of the cliff. Somehow he succeeded in dragging himself to its base and there he stayed.

His wife, meanwhile, did not miss him when he failed to return. She had no idea where he might have disappeared to. Nobody else, for that matter, knew where he was. His ill-behaved wife thus, when her husband did not show up, spent her nights with all sorts of men. Every time it turned dark, she would sleep with somebody else. She really was getting her fill of kwasi. At no time was she worried where her husband was. It never even occurred to her to search for him, for the boys and men continued seeking her out to have sex with her.

Quite a bit of time passed until the man got well again. He had recovered to the point where he felt no pain any longer. However, since he had badly injured his back, he had a hump now. He remembered Badger's instructions. Reflecting upon them he said to himself, "I'll go back to her." With that he took a trail up the cliff leading to the mesa top. Once there, he headed straight for home. It was late evening when he arrived. Somewhere along the way he picked some flowers, for it was summer, and came back to his wife with flowers in his arms. She recognized him at once. When he noticed that she was glad to see him back, he went up to her and held the flowers out to her. Playing with her in this way, the man ran away as his wife grabbed for the flowers. She kept chasing her husband around inside her house.

The man, of course, had taken the medicine Badger had given him before his homecoming, and he had arrived in a mood for sex. For this reason he teased his wife with the flowers. She pursued him all over, reaching for them, and finally wrested them away from him. No sooner had she put them down somewhere than her husband grabbed her and started making advances to her. So aroused had he been at the time he arrived that he immediately started copulating with his wife. Being the man-crazed woman that she was, she was elated. Consequently, the two had intercourse there all day long. Finally, it became evening and they had supper. As soon as they were done, they went to bed. But the man did not let his wife sleep. He really worked on her and coupled with her all night long. By the time the morning dawned his wife was finally satiated. She couldn't take any more. Evidently, her husband had become so potent that he did not let her sleep. And so both made it to the new day.

The man had also received another medicine from Badger. This one was pulverized and he had been instructed to sprinkle it into his wife's löwa. The

Figure 8: San Juan River region fluteplayers
Numerous fluteplayer images occur in clusters at sites along the San Juan River. Depicted as stick figures, the fluteplayer images are occasionally ithyphallic (b, d, h) and often humpbacked (c, d, e). Elaboration of the depictions is rare, although feathers (a)

man had done so just before they were going to have intercourse one last time. As a result, she became crazy when morning came. Evidently, she did not feel well when she woke up and could not bear to sit still. It was after midday when the woman went raving mad. First she tore off all her clothes. Then she ran to the same place where her husband had jumped off the cliff. Hurling herself down, the poor wretch died instantly. This is how her husband got his revenge.

From that day on the man lived alone, but the women kept flocking to him on their own accord. He really enjoyed them because he was so potent now. Due to his hump he became known as Kookopölö. Wherever he looked, there were girls around him. So whenever he danced, he would sing the following song:

Kookopölölö, Kookopölölö
Having a hump but always helping the women.
Kookopölölö, Kookopölölö
His hump being filled with helpfulness.
I have my water jug in my hump.
Kookopölölö, to the Paavön girl
became as a shade, came as a shade.
Vövövö.

Kookopölölö, Kookopölölö
Old man, old man.
Kookopölölö, Kookopölölö
Old man, old man.
Give me a water vessel.
Kookopölölö, old man.
Aayay vövö, aayay vövö.
Vövö, vövövövö.

From that time on the women kept seeking him out all by themselves. And he, having intercourse with them, got them pregnant. Meanwhile, the number of children was increasing because of Kookopölö. There was not a woman who had not borne a child by him. The boys and men were not happy at all that Kookopölö alone was enjoying all the girls. They were flocking to him only, so in a way he had them all as wives.

One day a young woman gave birth to a child. It was a girl and Kookopölö was the father. At this point the Turd People decided to put him to the test. The woman who had borne Kookopölö's child was extremely beautiful, the prettiest girl in the entire village. It was no wonder the Turds were jealous. They insisted that the baby girl was not Kookopölö's offspring and intended to take his wife away. They informed the couple about this and encouraged all the menfolks to descend to the plain below the mesa and pick a flower. The baby girl would be the daughter of the man whose flower she accepted.

A date was set, and when the appointed day arrived, the Turds went down and picked the most beautiful flowers, until there was not a pretty flower left anywhere. Kookopölö, poor thing, thus came back with just a single one of the flower called painted cup.

As the men ascended to the mesa top, the beautiful girl sat by the edge with her little girl in her arms. Whenever one of the Turds came by, he held out his flower to the infant, but she didn't so much as turn her head toward it. And she never reached out for what was held toward her.

Kookopölö was the very last to climb up, with his painted cup in his hand. The moment he arrived and held out the flower to the little girl, she grabbed for it. This made the Turds really jealous. Thus it appeared that the child was Kookopölö's, but they still did not approve of him having that beautiful girl. He should not have her. Somehow they would try to get rid of him. How could he love her, humpbacked creature that he was? Nor in any way was he lovable. Here he was, a homely and useless man, and yet the girl had given in to him. This is how the Turds criticized Kookopölö.

But things remained as they were. And since Kookopölö also was a hard-working farmer, the girl who had married him and had borne the child for him did not suffer any need. Though he had children by many others, he did not marry them but stayed only with this girl. The other women were heartbroken about this. Kookopölö's new wife was not as sex-hungry as his first and therefore remained with him. From that time on he did not succumb to any other women whenever they had the urge to have intercourse with him. So the couple lived together in peace.

The Turds could not stand seeing the girl married to Kookopölö and were constantly thinking of doing something to him. Repeatedly they tested him, but somehow he survived all their schemes. All those who planned to harm him failed in their endeavors, and died. Eventually, they had no choice but to give up and leave him alone. And so the population at Qa'ötaqtipu grew. Since all the children were Kookopölö's, there was a great number of his children living there. For this reason the Turds finally let go of him. They did not molest him anymore, and since he was an industrious farmer, he in a way provided for all of the people there. He's probably still living there somewhere. And here the story ends.

The Long Kwasi of Kookopölö

Aliksa'i. They were living in Oraibi. A great number of people was settled there, among them a couple that had just one daughter. She was extremely beautiful, and the young men desperately craved her love. Surprisingly enough, however, the girl did not care for any of them. The well-to-do boys constantly and in various ways tried to gain her love, but to no avail. With all sorts of things they attempted to gain her favor, but she didn't succumb to anyone. She didn't give in, yet the men were persistent and did not stop making advances to her.

Kookopölö, too, lived somewhere in the vicinity of Oraibi with only his grandmother. One day he also heard about the girl who rejected all her wooers, so he turned to his grandmother and said, "Grandmother, here in Oraibi lives a girl who doesn't love anyone. It occurred to me that I might try my luck with her." This is what he said.

His grandmother laughed at him. "You poor fool," she replied, "how could she take a fancy to someone as homely as you? She has rejected men much more handsome than you." This is what she said to her grandchild, teasingly laughing at him a little.

"Well, there's no harm in trying," Kookopölö responded. "I simply have to do it. The girl just might fall in love with me."

The girl had made it a habit of going to relieve herself every day at noon. For this purpose she went to the northeast side of Oraibi. There she relieved herself and then climbed back up the mesa. Each time she did exactly the same. Kookopölö was aware of this and was wondering whether he should perhaps just follow her to that place and grab her.

One dark night he was lying in bed again, racking his brain as to what he could possibly do to get the girl. Then it occurred to him, "Well, every day at noon she goes to the dump on the northeast side to relieve herself." This thought gave him an idea. That very same night he dug a ditch from his house all the way to the dump. Having completed the excavation in the course of just one night, he installed a reed which reached exactly to the spot where the girl came to defecate. Then he covered up the reed with earth and carefully removed all traces of his activity. The area looked as if nothing had happened. This is what Kookopölö did.

Then it became daylight. He now had to wait until noon. Sure enough, exactly at midday the girl came out of her house. He watched her carefully as she left, headed in the direction of the dump. Indeed, was Kookopölö excited and full of anticipation! When the girl had disappeared and gone down the mesa side, he pulled out his erect kwasi, and began inserting it into the reed. It was so long was it that it reached all the way to the end of the reed.

By this time the girl had arrived at her destination and squatted down. Apparently she didn't take anything off, and was squatting there, defecating. She was still in that position, when something pleasant began to happen in her löwa. It was a nice sensation, and when she looked, she was quite amazed to see something in it. But since it was so pleasant, she didn't do anything about it. Instead, she squatted there all excited, moving her body against the thing in her löwa.

Kookopölö, in turn, was busy working away with his kwasi from the other end of the reed near his house. He was almost beside himself. This is how he felt. Finally he had his orgasm, whereupon he pulled his kwasi back out. The girl also had a most pleasant experience.

Because of this enjoyable experience, the girl continued going there to relieve herself. And, indeed, each time she went to the dump the same thing happened to her. Out of the ground something would enter her löwa. Someone was having intercourse with her, but she never felt like resisting. Every time both Kookopölö and she had a good time.

Finally the girl became pregnant, and pretty soon her big belly was showing, whereupon her father said to her mother, "I wonder who got our child pregnant. She doesn't go with anyone and yet she is pregnant."

The young men also heard the news and were asking themselves how this could have happened. "Who could have gotten her pregnant? She never gives in to anyone, and here she is with child." This is what the young men were saying.

In due time the girl gave birth to a child even though she had no husband. Her parents were quite unhappy about this. Her father kept pondering this. She had to have borne this child for someone. He was set on finding out, and so he decided that the young men should have a race. He had the time of the race publicly announced and all the rules spelled out. The participants were to race and then pick a flower. Having picked the flower, each runner was supposed to bring it home, run to the girl's house, and offer it to his daughter's little child. Whoever offered a flower the child would accept would be its father. This is what the girl's father decided.

There were many young men anxious to participate, for after all, they stood a chance of winning a beautiful wife. When the day for the event arrived, the girl's father outlined every detail of his plan to the young men. Having had explained to them exactly what they were expected to do, they all took off running.

Evidently, Kookopölö heard that a race was taking place over that girl. Immediately, he informed his grandmother that he was going to participate. She responded with teasing laughter and said, "You won't catch up with anyone in that race. You're too much of a slowpoke."

Kookopölö, however, was determined to compete with them. He left the house, went to the place where the Oraibi men had raced off, and set out in pursuit of them. He was running along somewhere, when some of the runners began passing him from the opposite direction, returning home. Each one had some kind of flower in his hand, as the rules required. No sooner did each of the runners arrive than he headed straight for the girl's house and held out his flower to the little child. The baby rejected every flower. One after the other the runners tried, but without success.

Some time later Kookopölö also picked a flower and turned back toward the village. When he arrived at the mesa top, he made his way to the house of the girl. He still had not quite reached the house, when the little child became all excited and waved its hands about. No sooner had Kookopölö entered than the child went wild, craving the flower. The instant Kookopölö held out the flower, the little boy snatched it away from him.

When the girl's father saw this, he was dismayed but said, "All right, there's nothing I can do now; this is the way I wanted it. Since it was my wish to do this, I can't change my mind; this is how it's going to be." This is what he said to Kookopölö. So from that time on he had Kookopölö as a son-in-law.

The young men grew angry. How could the girl love such a creature! The

Turds, the denizens of Kwitavi, the Excrement Place, grew especially mad. They held a meeting and discussed how they might take Kookopölö's wife away from him. Carefully they deliberated on a pretext to get him into their kiva. Finally, they decided to simply invite him. When he arrived there they would be spinning wool. Later at midnight they would say that they were going to eat. Then while eating they would extinguish all the fires and kill him. This is the plan that the Turds devised for Kookopölö.

Kookopölö evidently learned about this scheme. He went to his grandmother and told her what he had heard. "Grandmother," he said, "I found out that the Turds are going to invite me to their kiva one of these days. There they want to kill me." This is what he told her.

"I knew it," his grandmother exclaimed. "They were bound to do that since you wouldn't give in and let the girl go. Don't waste any time now; hurry to Old Spider Woman." This is how she counseled him.

So Kookopölö went to Old Spider Woman. Upon his arrival at her place, she politely welcomed him. Then she said, "Well, you must have a purpose for visiting."

"Yes, of course," he answered. "Quite recently, as you may recall, the young men of Oraibi had a race about a girl. When I turned out to be the winner, the Turds were not pleased with the outcome. They have now plotted to kill me." This is what he said.

"Dear me," Old Spider Woman cried, "I will certainly help you. If they ever invite you to go with them, don't object but simply go along. First you'll be working at their kiva together with them. Later when they're going to start with their plan, they will say that they are going to have supper. Once you're eating, someone will extinguish the fire!"

Old Spider Woman, of course, is said to be such a supernatural being that she already knew all of this. She now brought out a bundle and rummaged around in it. After a while she pulled out something small, held it out to Kookopölö and said, "Here, this is powerful." He took it from her, and after inspecting it, noticed that he had been given some medicine. Old Spider Woman now continued, "Before the Turds extinguish the fire, chew this. Once the lights are out, spray this with your mouth in the darkness of the kiva. Then attach yourself to a spot on the ceiling. At that time it will be their turn." These were all the instructions she gave to him.

"All right, thanks indeed," Kookopölö replied, whereupon he returned home with his medicine.

It was dark night when he arrived. After bedding down with the girl, his wife, he enjoyed making love to her. Having done that he embraced her nicely and fell asleep with her. This time he had not used the reed.

And indeed, about two days later, someone called on Kookopölö. He had come to ask him along. "Why don't you come to our kiva?" he said. "We're going to spin yarn, so come and join us."

"All right, I'll come in a minute," Kookopölö replied.

When the other had left, Kookopölö grabbed his spindle and followed him. He entered the Turds' kiva. What a huge crowd of men there was! Sure enough, they spent the whole day spinning yarn, and Kookopölö, with his hump sticking out, was among them. Meanwhile it had gotten evening, and then dark night. Still the men continued spinning. Kookopölö, of course, was a stranger in their midst, because this was not his kiva. But even though he had realized this right away, he did not say a word. They thought he could not know what they had in store for him, so they kept busy spinning their wool. Finally, when it turned midnight, the one in charge of the spinning party announced, "All right, this should about do it. Let's eat and then we'll go to bed." This is what he told them.

The food that they were going to have had already been prepared, so they spread the meal out on the floor and everybody sat down. At this moment Kookopölö quickly shoved the medicine in his mouth and chewed it up, ahead of time as advised. They had just started eating, when someone extinguished the fire. No sooner did that happen than Kookopölö spurted forth his medicine and jumped right up to the ceiling. There he clung tightly to a beam until he attached himself to it. Once more he sprayed his medicine, this time down on the men. As a result, all of them got humped backs.

Now whenever one of the men happened to touch somebody else in the dark, and that person turned out to have a hump, he struck him with all his might. Thus, they were all furiously beating one another in the dark. Some even died from the blows. Eventually, someone shouted, "Something is not right. We all have humps, and some of us are lying on the floor. Start the fire back up."

So the Turds got the fire going again, and, true enough, they all had humped backs. Some of the men lay scattered around dead. Others were lying around with severe injuries they had inflicted upon themselves. Kookopölö, on the other hand, who all along had been nicely glued to the ceiling, now came back down.

This is how the Turds fared there. They had really wrought havoc on themselves. They now had to admit, "Well, he's no ordinary being, he really is endowed with supernatural powers. Therefore I'm sure he'll stay married to that girl, whether we like it or not."

Thus they failed to take Kookopölö's wife away, and he left the kiva and went home. The Turds, who are sorcerers, managed to transform themselves again, for they came back to life. Somehow they restored themselves, but not much later all of them perished. Whenever one of them tripped or hit against something, he died immediately.

This is how Kookopölö, with the help of Old Spider Woman, killed all the members of Kwitavi, the Excrement Place. He probably still has his beautiful wife. And most likely he also has a lot of children. And here the story ends.

Figure 9: Rio Grande River Valley fluteplayers
Large numbers of fluteplayer images occur at several sites in the upper Rio Grande River Valley. The images, believed to be quite late (post A.D. 1200 to as late as A.D. 1600), are elaborate, virtually all full-figured, often ithyphallic (d, f, h), and generally humpbacked (a, d, f, h, k, l). The elaboration of fluteplayer figures includes enlarged feet (a) and headdresses (d, e, f, i, j, l).

The Orphan Boy and His Wife

Aliksa'i. People were living in Oraibi. Long ago many people called this village their home. Among them was a boy who had lost his parents. He lived all alone, without even a grandmother to depend on. Hence there was nobody to instruct him how to act. When someone has a grandmother, one learns many things from her.

So he lived all by himself as an orphan. In addition, he had no friends and never visited anybody. Whatever he did, he kept to himself. As he grew older, he started hunting for game. In those days, the ancient ones used to eat the meat of cottontails and jackrabbits as well as that of big animals such as antelope and deer. The boy, who was just an adolescent, did not really know how to stalk big game, so he only hunted cottontails and jackrabbits. Only these he ate. And because he knew how to roast them, he did not eat them raw. When someone is an orphan, one does things the way one experiences them, and since he was an orphan, he lived like one.

Of course, there were girls and women around him; also boys and men. But he had no desire to mix with them. He was a loner by nature. Long ago boys used to compete in various activities and play with each other. But he always avoided others. Being without parents, he actually was afraid of people. Not thinking much of himself and timid at heart, he did not participate with others. For this reason, he also had no interest in girls. He should have had fun with them. However, no one was telling him that he should enjoy the girls. And because that was the case, he just lived the way he was. He also stayed away from all public events, such as kachina or social dances. He did whatever he pleased. In this fashion he grew to be a young man, roaming the land far and wide.

As time passed, a young woman got to know him. Apparently, she took a fancy to him, because she would go to his place. In doing so she got him interested in herself. In the end he gave in to her and they decided to get married, but the poor boy had no idea how to provide her with a wedding outfit. After all, he had no one to depend on. Somehow, though, they talked it over and got married. Now they were living together.

As it turned out, the man had no desire to sleep with his wife. Whenever it was bed time, he made all kinds of excuses for not coming to bed until later. He had learned the skill of weaving, and that was what he was doing. When one engages in weaving, one usually has to card wool deep into the night. This is how a weaver spends his nights. The same is true after one starts spinning. And since this man spun a lot, he would sleep only a short time before it became daylight. Normally, it was deep into the night before he came to bed. Each time his wife wanted them to go to bed early, he would say to her, "Why don't you go ahead of me? I won't sleep for a while yet. I need to work on this. I'll come to bed after I've spun a lot."

His wife, who desired her husband, had no choice but to lie down. For hours the poor woman would lie waiting, but when her husband failed to join her, she usually fell asleep. For this reason, being married to this man was not very enjoyable for her. He simply would not have sex with her. People say that some women want to have sex a lot and really long for it. That woman was like that. And since she was not satisfied sexually, she was thinking of divorcing her husband. The man, who had grown up so inexperienced, never gave this matter much thought. He really had no idea how to have intercourse with his wife. No one had ever explained to him how to take care of a woman. Being totally unfamiliar with these things, he did not know how to sleep with his wife. This is how he lived there.

The woman became resentful toward her husband and did not want him in her house any more. Her love for him began to decline. The man, apparently, began to notice this. He kept thinking that if someone could enlighten him and he could learn how to have intercourse with a woman, he could then do it to his wife.

One day someone told him about Kookopölö. He explained that Kookopölö lived in Oraibi somewhere and could take care of his problem. He was in the habit of administering erection medicine. Without fail, any man who received the medication got interested in sex. Also, if a woman wanted a child, she would pray to Kookopölö. He answered the women's prayers and gave them children.

For some time the man thought about what he had been told. Finally, he asked someone where this Kookopölö lived. He decided to seek him out, so one evening he said to his wife, "Tonight I won't be carding wool for a while. I want to go somewhere."

His wife had no objections. "All right, you go wherever you want to go," she replied.

After the two had eaten supper, the man left the house and went in search of Kookopölö. Upon arrival at his place he entered. Kookopölö welcomed the visitor and had him sit down. Then he said, "Well, there's got to be a reason you're about at this time of night."

"Yes," answered the man, "I came to consult with you on a problem I have."

"Well, what problem is that?"

The man explained, "I have a wife. But because I grew up not practicing intercourse with any girl and also am a loner by nature, I don't know how to have sex. Maybe you can show me so that when I get into the mood, I can have sex with her. It seems she doesn't love me any more. I've noticed that she resents me in the house. If I could learn to have sex with her, I could sleep with her. As you know, there is a saying, 'A man should have sex with his wife.' But I, for one, am not doing that."

To this Kookopölö replied, "It's true, I do prescribe remedies for people in these matters. I want you to get a rooster when you get home. Once you have one, shell some corn and store the kernels in a bag. Then come back with both. Also bring your wife along. If you come in four days, I'll show you what you need to do."

"Very well, I'll certainly do that," the man said.

With that he returned home. It was dark night by the time he arrived. Upon entering he noticed that his wife was asleep again. As before, he bedded down next to her and went to sleep without touching her.

The following morning he pondered where he could acquire a rooster. When it got daylight he had breakfast, and set out. He knew a man who had domestic animals, so he headed over to his place. Without asking the owner's permission, he entered his chicken pen and started chasing the fowl. There were lots of roosters. He grabbed one of them and carried it home.

After bringing the rooster home, he bundled it up and placed it in a bag, where he kept it. Then he said to his wife, "Please shell about four ears of corn.

Put the kernels in a bag, for tomorrow we'll take them to Kookopölö. I visited with him a couple of nights ago. He told me to get some corn and a rooster and then come see him together with you."

His wife did as bidden. After shelling the ears, she bagged the kernels, and early the next day the two started forth. Upon reaching their destination, they found Kookopölö already waiting for them. "You've come?" he greeted them.

"Yes," the husband and wife replied. "And this is what we brought." With that the man handed Kookopölö the rooster.

Upon also receiving the corn, Kookopölö said, "All right, let's not waste any time." At first he administered the stiffening medicine to the man. When one does that, one must under no circumstance have the person swallow it. Instead, it is to be spread on the body. Should someone eat the medicine, the stiff kwasi will not go down anymore and a man will die as a result. So Kookopölö insisted that the medicine not be taken internally. It's always smeared on the lower back and around the waist. This is exactly what Kookopölö did.

Thereupon Kookopölö said, "Let me know when your little boy is all the way up. Then we can begin."

Before long, the man's kwasi was good and stiff. So he said to Kookopölö, "It's standing up now."

"Very well. Come over here, both of you." With that he rolled out some bedding for the man and his wife. "You lie down here," he bade the man's wife. The woman did as told. Kookopölö now turned to the man and said, "You lie with your stomach on top of her. Then put your kwasi into her löwa. When it goes in, it will go directly into the hole," he explained.

The two did as told. The man placed himself on top of his wife and inserted his kwasi into her löwa. Next, Kookopölö scattered the corn kernels on the man's back. Having done that, he placed the rooster on top of him. No sooner had he done so than the rooster was busy eating. He kept pecking the man, of course, and every time he hit him with its beak, the man jerked his pelvis. The rooster hurt him, so he kept thrusting into his wife. Eventually, he was getting the hang of it. Before long, he was able to move his pelvis by himself, and soon had his climax. His wife, who finally experienced intercourse with him, was elated.

This is how Kookopölö showed the couple how to have sex. The rooster, meanwhile, had gobbled up all of the kernels. The man now climbed off his wife, and when the latter had gotten up, Kookopölö said, "This is how one does it to one's wife. From now on the two of you can work on this. You're bound to get stiff," he assured the man.

"Thank you, indeed," replied the man. "It's just that I didn't know how before."

"I'm sure you'll be making your wife happy from now on," Kookopölö said.

This is how the couple fared there, and then they went home. From that day on the man would lie down early at night with his wife. As soon as he had an erection, he climbed on top of her. Having sex in this way, the woman got pregnant. Soon she gave birth to a child and gave up her plans to divorce her husband. Because Kookopölö had given the man the medication and he now regularly had intercourse with his wife, she held on to him. They now had sex like all the other married people and for this reason they had children. And here the story ends.

The Crying Cicada

Aliksa'i. People were living in Oraibi and in other settlements all across the land.

Long ago, the people of Oraibi used to eat all sorts of living things. For example, they made stew out of cottontails and jackrabbits. The same was true for antelopes that roamed the area in those days. To hunt bigger game such as deer, the Oraibis trekked all the way to Nuvatukya'ovi, the San Francisco Mountains. If they were lucky enough to bag a deer, they made a meal out of it too. Once in a while they even brought back a large elk. All these animals they used to cook and eat.

And the cicadas were also part of their diet. In the olden days, it was usually very hot in the vicinity of the Hopi villages, so cicadas appeared in great abundance. Apparently, someone long ago had tried the taste of them and found it to his liking. As a result, people started eating cicadas regularly. And since the insects come out when it is hot, they used to be right out in the open there when the heat of summer was upon the land. Hence, someone who wanted cicadas would go hunt for them when the weather was hot. Upon bringing some home, a woman made fire under a cooking pot. The cicadas were then cast into the pot and roasted. In those days the cooking vessels were normally made out of clay.

There was also an old woman living in Oraibi. Once when she was at a loss as to what to cook for the family, she bade all her grandchildren go hunt cicadas. As soon as the sun was a little up in the sky, the children went down from the mesa to the plain and hunted around. Sure enough, as the air was getting warmer, the chirping of the cicadas could be heard clearly. Whenever one of the insects was singing somewhere, one of the children would try to sneak up to it, moving along, aiming for the spot where the chirping came from. If he succeeded in locating the exact spot, he would reach out for the insect and catch it if he was lucky. This is what the children were doing there now. One of them, who was not as old as the others, followed them around with a bag into which they put the cicadas.

In the village, meanwhile, the old woman got the cooking pot ready. After all, it was close to noontime. She already had a small fire going under the vessel ahead of the children's arrival. When it was about time for the hunters to come home, she added a lot of fuel and soon had a good fire going. Just when her pot got really warmed up, the children arrived and handed the cicadas over to their grandmother. They had caught a great many and the old woman was elated. "Oh, thank you! Now we can have a feast. I'm so glad you're old enough to go get these critters," she exclaimed, thanking her grandchildren. With that she carried the cicadas to the cooking pot and threw them in alive. For that is how one roasts them. After dumping them in the pot, she closed the pot with a sifter basket, stirring all the while.

The old woman was still busy doing that when one of the cicadas somehow managed to crawl out from under the sifter. It flew away from the woman and settled down not far from her. The poor thing had been burned on one side, so it squatted there crying.

Tsiiriiriirii,
Tsiiriiriirii.
Cottontails and jackrabbits
Used to be good meat·for a stew.
But now we taste the best.
Tsiiriiriirii.

This is how the cicada wept.

The old woman heard something. Listening closely, she could barely make out a voice somewhere near her. Investigating the area next to her, she finally saw it. There beside her was a flat rock, and on it had landed the cicada she had heard talking. She paid close attention to what it was saying. Finally she exclaimed, "Oh my, poor thing! Did you not get roasted with the others? Yes, you are very delicious. That's why we eat you. Sure, there are cottontails and jackrabbits out there, but they're very swift and good runners. That's why we don't get to eat too many of them. And because we enjoy how you taste, we're eating you too," she said to the cicada.

Reproaching the old woman, the cicada replied, "You know very well that the weather gets warm because of us, and yet you eat us."

"Oh dear, that's right, we get warm weather because of you and here we are killing you," the woman admitted.

"Yes, indeed," the cicada continued. "The minute I get home I'll tell the others, and then the weather won't warm up so early any more. Anyway, it's up to you. From this day on you can have winter when summer comes around. We're the only ones who know all about the heat, and look how you treat us."

"Oh dear, oh dear! I'll tell my people that we won't do that anymore," the old woman wailed.

"Well, since you are like this, we're thinking of moving somewhere else. All you do is kill us, which is wrong."

"I'm sorry, indeed. I assure you, we won't eat you any more. And we won't be killing you any longer. We need you to warm up the land for us early in the year, so we can plant early and not have a hard time with our crops. When we have crops to eat, we don't need to hunt you any more."

The cicada, however, had grown so angry that it flew off without a response. It returned to the others, thinking that after telling them about its experience they would leave the area so the Hopis could not eat and kill them any longer. Upon reaching home it assembled the cicadas and spoke to them this way, "If we quit living here, they can't devour us any more."

The fall season was just about upon them as it spoke these words. And so the cicadas had departed when the weather turned cold. Since they normally leave around this time, none of the Hopis gave it much thought. All of the cicadas, however, had agreed to stop living there. They were unanimous in their decision and acted accordingly.

Thereafter, whenever summer rolled around, the weather simply would not get hot. The land did not warm up properly. Way back when lots of cicadas had made their home there, it always was hot during that season. There had usually been great numbers of them there, making their chirping sounds. But now after the cicada had told its people what it had learned and they had departed, the weather did not get as hot as before. It would still get comfortably warm, but by no means was the temperature as hot. And so the land failed to warm up early in the year, and the crops were late in maturing. When the people became aware of this, they did not eat as many cicadas as they used to, especially the old people who had some brains. They wanted the cicadas to return.

One man in particular, who was in charge of some ceremony, had been mulling this situation over. He thought that if he fashioned pahos with the cicadas and prayed to them, they might consider coming back. So he went out hunting for them and killed a few. He poked them on a stick, storing them for later. As he made his pahos then, he attached one of the dead insects on the prayer stick. Then he uttered the following prayer, "I wish you, cicadas, would have pity on us and return from where you went. Then it could get nice and warm again early in the season." Then he added, "And maybe it would be all right if we eat you. You see, we got to like the taste of you and now need you for our sustenance." This is the prayer he spoke, whereupon he deposited the paho with some cornmeal.

Evidently the cicadas consented, for they returned. Now the weather got hot early in the year once more. As before, the people ate them, but this time the insects did not leave. Thus, in spite of using them as food again, the Hopis harvested their crops early. From that day on they also made prayer sticks with cicadas. Whenever one does so, the weather quickly gets nice and warm. The cicadas, in turn, never returned to the place they had come back from. For this reason prayer sticks are still being fashioned during the Flute ceremony.

And here the story ends.

a

b

c

d

e

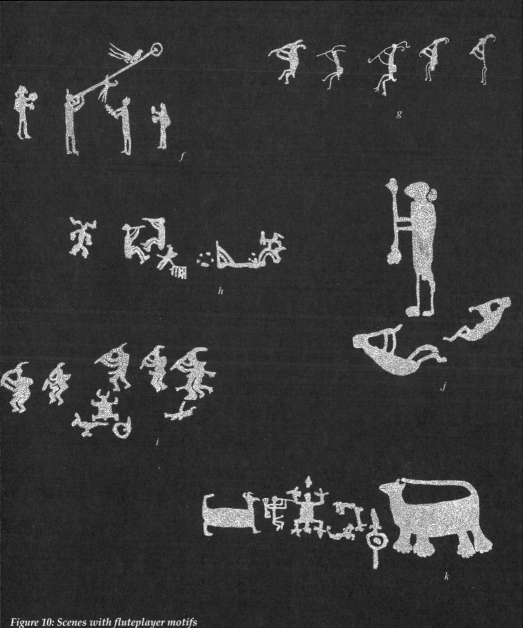

Figure 10: Scenes with fluteplayer motifs
Compositions or scenes in which one or several fluteplayers figure prominently (e, f, g, h, i, j) are found throughout the American Southwest. Game animal associations (a, b) may point to a direct connection between the fluteplaying images and magical control of the animals. Other contexts are enigmatic (c, d), including a rare scene in which a fluteplayer is being carried by another figure (d). In some scenes the fluteplayers dominate because of their size (e, f, g, h, i), while in others, they appear subordinate and tiny (c, d, j, k).

The Cicadas and the Serpents

Aliksa'i. Many people were living at Oraibi and there were settlements all across the land. At a place called Tsu'akpi all kinds of serpents, including rattlesnakes, had made their home. When it got to be summer and the weather turned warm, they would roam the land as serpents are accustomed to do. But in winter time they were all underground, where they would transform themselves into human shape. To do so they simply shed their skins and hung them from a peg on the wall of their house.

At Tuuwanasavi the cicadas were at home. Some of them were the colorful kind, others were white as clay. Just like the serpents at Tsu'akpi, they all lived together in one place.

One day long ago, a blizzard had been blowing, and now the ground was covered with a great deal of snow. It had never snowed this much before at the beginning of the cold season. Everything was buried in snow, and the land was white as far as the eye could reach. Since the sun was barely shining, it was bitterly cold.

Already the wood supplies of the people were giving out, and still the weather was not getting any warmer. The snow, which simply would not melt, also prevented the people from going after wood. More than one tried, but they did not get far before they became exhausted from plodding through the deep snow. The freezing weather also continued. From one point on they hardly had any wood left. Finally, some people actually froze to death.

By contrast, the area where the cicadas lived was free of snow. They possessed the knowledge of warm weather and heat and for this reason were always comfortably warm in their homes.

The serpents were not accustomed to the cold either and began freezing to death. So their headman assembled his strongmen and said to them, "How terrible! We can't go on like this. It just doesn't get warm, and because we can't get out and hunt around, we've used up all our food. We're starving to death and dying from the cold. Therefore I suggest that one of us who still has some strength left seek out the cicadas. When he gets there, he can plead with them to have mercy on us and let the weather get warm. But we're not only

asking for ourselves. There must be others out there praying for warmth."
This is what he said, whereupon one serpent expressed his willingness to take
on this task.

It was Sandsnake that had volunteered. "I can give it a try at least," he
said. With that he slipped into his skin, thereby transforming himself into a
sandsnake again. He did not intend to make the journey in his human shape.
And so he left the house and started forth. However, he had not yet reached
his destination when he became tired and so cold that he was forced to turn
around. By the time he returned home he was completely exhausted.

The headman bade someone else try, for they couldn't go on living under
these conditions. Only if it got warm could they recover. This time a big bullsnake volunteered. "I can give it a try at least," he said.

"Yes, indeed, try your luck," said the headman. "You're very strong and
might get there. I'm afraid it's been cold so long now that it doesn't seem that
it will ever warm up again," he said, encouraging Bullsnake to be strong on
his journey.

Bullsnake also dressed in his skin, leaving the house and heading out in
the direction of Tuuwanasavi. True enough, it was biting cold. No wonder the
first one, poor thing, almost froze to death before it returned. Bullsnake had
barely left his home when he met the fierce north wind. But he mustered up
his courage and moved along. He knew that under the present conditions they
would die soon, so he kept striving on through the deep snow. At least he
made it somewhat farther than Sandsnake, but in the end he also got exhausted before he could reach his goal. He, too, poor wretch, was forced to cut
short his journey and return home.

The older serpents were unhappy when they heard that he had not succeeded, but they did not reprimand him for his failure. After all, it was extremely cold outside. Someone else would have to venture forth, though.

Before anybody said anything, Whipsnake spoke up. "I'll go. I alone will
be able to get through the snow. You two are heavier than I. That's why you
sank in. If I move along on the surface of the snow, I might make it there." He
was already dressing as he spoke.

As soon as Whipsnake had his skin on he departed. The temperature was
as cold as before, and there seemed to be no sign of the sun. Thick clouds en-

gulfed the entire sky, rolling in big waves toward the northeast. The ice cold northwest wind was also not letting up. It occurred to Whipsnake that he might not reach Tuuwanasavi, but he was not willing to turn around. He might not succeed in locating the cicadas, but he was going to continue on braving the north wind. He grew a little angry with himself for volunteering, but it just wouldn't do to head back. It was his own fault that he had volunteered. He didn't want to embarrass himself, so he struggled on.

Whipsnake climbed on top of the snow, and since he was very light, he slithered along quite nicely. In addition, he was an excellent runner, which allowed him to move along quite forcefully. He knew he was nearing his destination when the air began to get warmer. No longer freezing and somewhat strengthened by the warmth, he now moved along at a rapid pace.

Eventually Whipsnake reached the home of the cicadas, where there was a large area completely free of snow. Right in the center of this clearing stood a ladder protruding from under the ground. He headed toward it, for this had been the idea of coming here. By the time he arrived at his destination the air was gently warm. The ground was covered with green plants and flowers. He had just come through the severest winter and now here he was in the middle of summer. No wonder Whipsnake stared in amazement. How glad he was to have gotten here without falling victim to the cold. "Thanks, I arrived without harm," he said to himself.

He stood there listening. No doubt, the cicadas lived there. He climbed on the roof and called inside, "Hey! Isn't anybody home?"

True enough, they were there, for he heard a voice, "Sure, we're home. Come on in, stranger." Whipsnake entered and the cicadas welcomed him. Just as outside, the temperature was nice and warm inside their house, and they were living very comfortably there.

An old man, not wasting his time, bade Whipsnake to come over to the fire pit and smoke with him. Just as their smoking ritual was coming to an end, a few of the women were setting out some food for him. When they finished their smoke, the old man said to him, "All right, eat first. When you're full, you can share with us the reason for your visit." Whipsnake ate. All kinds of delicacies had been served. He ate watermelon, muskmelon, roasted corn, all the crops that normally grow only in the warm season. He was starved, so he really gorged himself.

When Whipsnake was full, he explained to everybody why he had come. He told the cicadas how they were suffering from the cold at home. "Two of us attempted to come here, but failed. The poor wretches were so frozen that they had to turn around. However, because I'm so light, I did not sink in the snow and that's how I managed to get here. Not many of us are alive any more, so I came to implore your help. We all know that you command the warm weather. Have mercy with us and let it get warmer earlier in the year again. Then we can leave our homes and set out in search of food."

The old cicada replied, "Is that so? I'm sorry, indeed. This must have happened because we've been so tardy. Go back and tell your people not to worry anymore. We'll set things right for you again. All this must have come to pass due to our tardiness. Go deliver this message now." And then he added, "As soon as you get home, tell them to wait for us in four days."

Upon receiving these instructions Whipsnake said, "Very well. I'll go back and deliver your words." As he was leaving, someone else spoke to him. "Wait a moment. I'll come with you. Then things will be different." Whipsnake stopped to wait.

The cicada that had spoken to him picked up a flute somewhere and said, "All right, let's go out together now."

With that the two climbed out on the roof. The cicada walked away from the kiva in a westerly direction, and then stopped. He held out his flute in the direction of the serpent's home and started to play. As he did so, a narrow lane, clear of snow, was forming all the way to his home. Apparently, the cicada was blazing a trail for him. Before long, there was a clear road all the way.

When the cicada was finished, he said, "All right, now you're bound to get to your house quickly. Go happily." Whipsnake set forth. Indeed, not much time passed and he was back. The other serpents were elated. They were convinced that he had been to the home of the cicadas. No sooner was he back than he related the cicadas' words. The serpents were glad to receive such good tidings.

Happy in their hearts, the serpents now waited for the coming of the cicadas on the fourth day. As best as they could, they cleaned up their house. When the appointed day arrived, they were full of expectations. They could not sit still any longer and were filled with joyful apprehension.

The sun had just started its slide down the horizon when the cicadas started out at Tuuwanasavi. One behind the other, they formed a long line on the way to the serpents. But they did not go as cicadas; rather, they came transformed as human beings, just like us. Each one carried a flute, had a bell tied around his hand, and was clad in a rabbit skin blanket.

The serpents could clearly hear the visitors as they were arriving. Upon reaching the serpents' home, the cicadas shook their rattles, and then the serpents invited them in. So many entered that they filled the entire kiva standing along the walls. Then they started dancing. And this is how their song went:

> Haw'o my mothers, haw'o my fathers.
> Gray Flute members, Blue Flute members our fathers.
> Beautiful life
> We will awaken.
> Aa'aa'aahaa, aa'aa'haa'aa, aayaa.
> Sunny we will make it.
> Through a bright and sunny day we will go along.
> Aa'aahaa'aa ii'iihii'ii'ii
> For sure
> Colorful cicadas, clay-white cicadas.
> Beautiful life
> We will awaken.
> Aa'aa'aahaa, aa'aa'haa'aa', aayaa.
> Sunny we will make it.
> Through a bright and sunny day we will go along.
> Aa'aahaa'aa, ii'iihii'ii'ii.

This is how the cicadas sang. And while they danced the temperature rose inside the kiva. By the time they finished the dance, the serpents were completely covered with sweat. The cicadas only staged one dance, then they filed out of the kiva. The serpents were grateful for the entertainment. After exiting the cicadas returned home.

All the way home the cicadas played their flutes. As they were walking along, the snow began to thaw. And not only along their trail. All across the land the snow was disappearing and the weather was warming up.

From that day on, everything on the land began to grow again and things started to bloom. Only after the cicadas had danced, and once more all life on earth was warm.

And here the story ends.

a

b

c

d

e

f

g

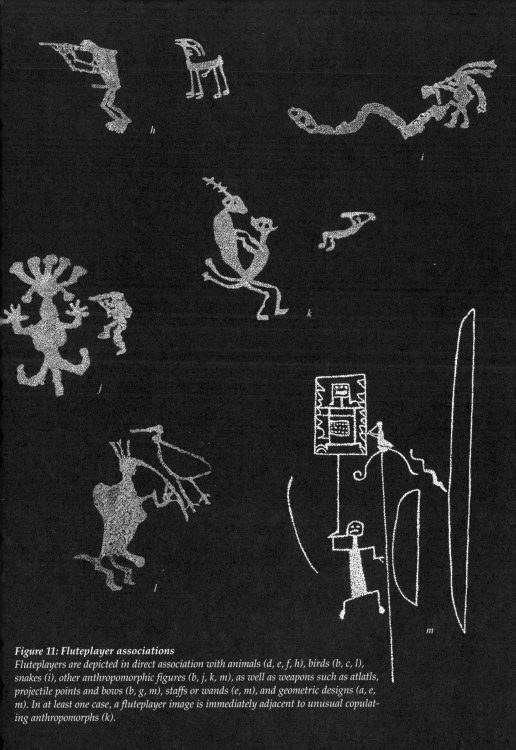

Figure 11: Fluteplayer associations
Fluteplayers are depicted in direct association with animals (d, e, f, h), birds (b, c, l), snakes (i), other anthropomorphic figures (b, j, k, m), as well as weapons such as atlatls, projectile points and bows (b, g, m), staffs or wands (e, m), and geometric designs (a, e, m). In at least one case, a fluteplayer image is immediately adjacent to unusual copulating anthropomorphs (k).

The Boy Who Went in Search of the Cicadas

Aliksa'i. They were living at Sikyatki. Long ago not many people lived at the village of Sikyatki, so they all knew one another. On certain occasions they would get together and practice their rituals. They would conduct their Wuw-tsim and Soyal rites and perform their Powamuy ceremony. They were carrying out all the Hopi rituals.

They also raised crops but their crops would not always fully mature. This had happened more than once. When summer came there would only be a short period of warmth before the weather turned cold again. In the end, this began to happen every year. The people said to themselves, "We're doing something wrong to make our crops turn out this way." This was what the leaders of Sikyatki thought, and they asked themselves, "Who is the being that has the knowledge of making it warm? Where could they go to seek him?" The earth would no longer warm up for any great length of time. Because of this, their crops froze before developing fully. So they decided to come together and ponder this matter. Perhaps they could seek out the one who could make heat.

When the time for the Soyal ceremony came, the head of the ritual set a date for it to begin. The town crier made the announcement accordingly. When the Soyal ceremony finally got under way, there was talk throughout the kivas about the crop failure. "It's been a long time since the earth has warmed up. As you remember, we decided that while undertaking this ritual we would seek the one who can produce heat. We made these plans and now the time has come. We're now about to make prayer feathers and prayer sticks. Perhaps we could also make some for the being who produces heat, and then someone could seek him out for us. Maybe if we prepare these things for him, he'll have pity on us and warm the earth for a longer time. So, to my thinking, we should get on it right away. I'll tell my son, then, to go out and look for that being. If luck is with us, and he goes about it the right way, he'll be able to locate him."

So the village leader chose his son for this task. He said to him, "We just set a date for Soyalangw. When that day comes, I want you to leave in search of this being. When you find him, ask him on our behalf to warm the earth so we may reap crops again."

As the appointed day grew near, the youth, along with the others in the village, fasted. He didn't eat salt. He also ate very skimpy meals because he was running to get himself in shape. His father had told him, "When one is running to become fit, such as you are, in order to stay light one must not eat big meals. So one should eat as little as possible."

From that point toward the appointed date, the son readied himself. Since his task was an important one, he really agreed to his father's request.

As time progressed, the son of the village leader grew stronger and stronger. One day his trainer said to him, "It is clear that you have reached the peak of your strength. You are now able to return home before the sun has risen. You no longer breathe hard when you overtake me. This is what your father wanted for you, so from now on you'll be on your own."

Meanwhile Soyalangw, the appointed date, had arrived. The boy's mother carefully prepared some journey food for him. She knew her son would be undertaking this task, so she had begun grinding some sweet corn into a fine meal. From this she fashioned tiny loaves of *qömi* which she then baked. When he was about to set out, she tied his journey food around his waist. "Take this along," she said. "I think this will be enough for you until you return. I've also included plenty of dried peaches. So you've got a good supply of food."

Meanwhile, his father had wrapped all their prayer feathers and prayer sticks into a brand new mantle, which he now slung over one of his son's shoulders and under the other, tying it at his chest. "These you must take along. Unfortunately, we cannot give you any directions, but whenever you come upon someone, tell them what you seek; perhaps they'll be able to tell you where the being lives who knows how to make heat. Just ask for directions as you move along since you're taking a good amount of prayer items with you. Give at least one to anyone who helps you find your way. But the largest number you must save for the one you seek. Don't run at your top speed all the way, don't put yourself to too much hardship. Wherever you are at evening, stop there, eat and rest, and then proceed onward the following day before the gray of the dawn appears over the horizon." With that he handed his son a canteen filled with water and said, "Pay close attention to your water. Water cannot be found everywhere. When one becomes thirsty, one suffers. If you don't eat a few times, it will do you no harm, but once your water is gone, you will face much difficulty. Whenever you get thirsty, take some water into your mouth, swish it around in there, and then swallow it. If you do this, you'll be able to go farther," he told him. Next he handed his son a flat, curved hunting stick and said, "All right, this is also for you. From this you will greatly benefit. There are cottontails and jackrabbits all over. Whenever you have the urge to eat meat, take this to knock your prey down. Then you can kill it and roast it for your meal."

That same morning the entire village gathered to wish the boy good luck on his trip. Miserable as they were, the people were hoping with all sincerity that he would find the being who knew how to produce heat so the days would get warmer. Everybody spoke words of encouragement to him and, for what good it might do, gave him of their sacred cornmeal. As he was about to leave, his father and the village headmen drew out a path of white cornmeal for him. After they finished this, the boy set out in a westerly direction.

Since long ago, whenever the ancient Hopis needed something, they would pray toward Pisisvayu [the Colorado River] and also toward Nuvatukya'ovi [the San Francisco Peaks]. Perhaps the boy could deposit the prayer items at one of these not-so-distant places and, while he was still there, the one whom he sought would approach him and would give him the information he wanted. He would then not have to travel such a vast distance, and at the same time he would achieve his goal and return home. With this in mind the youth began his journey west.

Since the boy did not have a particular destination in mind, he headed directly toward Pisisvayu. When he got there, he waited for someone to approach him, but when no one did, he went on to Nuvatukya'ovi. There he experienced the same. No one showed up, so he continued on his way.

Eventually he arrived at the west side of Nuvatukya'ovi. By then evening had fallen, and this was to be his first stop. He satisfied his hunger and lay down for the night.

The following morning, before the gray dawn appeared, he arose, ate some of his journey food, and went on his way. He did not run, but walked at a steady pace. He knew that by doing this he would not get too tired along the way. Following his father's instructions, whenever he got thirsty he would take a mouthful of water, walk along with it in his mouth, and swallow it after a little while. In this fashion he conserved his water supply and trekked along, farther and farther, resting only for the night.

One day at noon he had the urge to relieve himself, so he headed for a salt bush and squatted next to it. He had just begun to strain when he heard a voice say, "How awful, my grandchild. Don't do it there. Go a little bit farther off, then do it."

The boy obeyed and moved to another site. Once more he squatted, and this time no one protested. All the while he looked around the area, but did not see anyone. "I wonder who was speaking to me and from where?" he thought. When he was done, he returned to the place where he had heard the voice. Standing over this spot, much to his surprise, he saw an opening, and jutting out from it was a tiny ladder. He spoke into the hole, "There's no way I can get into your place. The opening is too small."

A voice replied, "Wiggle your heel in the hole and the opening will get wider." He did as told, and true enough, the entranceway opened and he was able to enter.

The voice now said, "Welcome, it is I who lives here. I have my house here."

The boy now noticed that it was an old woman who had welcomed him. "Have a seat, stranger," she said. Unmistakably, this was Old Spider Woman. It was she who had her abode there and who had asked why he was traveling about.

The boy said, "Yes, we in the Hopi country are farmers. We keep planting our crops and they sprout, but before our crops mature, they freeze. For a long time we've endured this. When fall arrives, we reap little. Now I've been sent to seek the one who has the power to make heat. This is as far as I have come."

"Goodness yes, that's the way things are out there at Hopi. I know all about it, and I felt sorry for you. That's why I revealed myself to you. I'll be going with you now," she said.

The boy was very happy when he learned that he would not have to go on his search alone. After all, he had no idea where to go, and the landscape was becoming more and more unfamiliar. He might venture through a thick forest and take a wrong turn even though the sun might still be visible.

From there on Old Spider Woman went with the boy. She told him that she would be riding on his ear as they went along. "Very well," the boy acknowledged, "you're certainly welcome to sit there while I walk. I won't mind. While you sit there, you can give me directions."

"Yes, and if something somewhere wants to put you to a test, I will see it first and let you know about it," she said.

"Very well," he answered, "I'm very happy. Yes, let's journey together."

The two now started forth. The old woman warned him, "They're bound to put you through some tests. Four times as a matter of fact. They will test you for your courage, but nothing will happen to you while I'm by your side. So don't be afraid when you meet danger, for by being together we'll somehow survive the ordeal."

Sure enough, they were traveling along somewhere when they saw a great cloud of dust in the west. Then the boy time kept an eye on the cloud of dust as he jogged along. "Someone is moving toward us," he said to the old woman.

"Yes, I know, so gather up your strength," she replied. "Be strong. That one ahead of you tends to become evil. When he's in a bad mood, he has no consideration for anyone. He's going to test your courage. But don't be frightened. You need not be afraid of him. When he stands before you, he'll ask you a question."

The dust cloud was approaching from the west with great speed. Apparently, it was a whirlwind. Finally, they were nearing each other. Lo and behold, there was a kiva there into which the whirlwind quickly vanished. The boy was not far away when this happened. Following the instructions of Old Spider Woman the boy quickly entered. The dust devil, meanwhile, had settled in a niche just above the floor at the north end of the chamber. He was an awful, hideous creature, and he was apparently very angry, for something was coming out of his nostrils.

The old woman whispered to the boy, "He won't harm you. He came only to scare you. There's a way out. Just go up to him without showing any fear. If he asks you something, answer him in full."

As predicted, the creature stood up, confronted the boy and asked, "You have just reached this place?"

"Yes," replied the boy.

Next the creature asked why he was about, and the boy told the entire story of his journey.

"I see. It's still quite a long way to your destination. I must admit, you are brave, for you have entered my home. I live here because I'm a guard. Evidently it was to be that if you entered my home, you would beat me."

The old lady whispered instructions to the boy. "You two must race each other. It was for this reason that your father had you practice running in the country every day, to build your strength. So now, give it all you have, and run as fast your legs will carry you."

The dust devil paced off a small distance and then drew a line on the ground. "All right," he said, "let's stand here side by side. The minute I shout Taa! we'll dash to the east. We'll circle that huge boulder over there. If you come back here before I do, you can pass through this place and continue your journey. But if I return before you, I will have to stop you."

Together the two came up to where the line had been drawn and stood side by side. As they did this, the youth glanced over at the whirlwind, but there was no whirlwind any more. He had transformed himself into a deer. So he was expected to compete with a deer. The deer now shouted Taa! and off they went with all the speed that each could muster. The youth had such great speed that he was soon ahead in the race, and the deer could not overcome him. As the boy returned to the home of the deer, he dashed past the starting line and went off to the other side.

When he did this he exclaimed, "Wow! It's amazing that I beat him." The deer now arrived, panting heavily. He just stood there with his tongue hanging out, breathing hard. His mouth was foaming and spittle was dripping from it. The deer finally got his breath and declared, "Hey, I thought I was fast, but you have beaten me, so go on happily toward your destination. However, at another place you'll encounter somebody else. He is far greater than I. He too gets quickly angry for almost no reason at all."

"Is that true?" the boy asked.

"Yes. All right, be on your way, for you have gotten the better of me," he said, and the boy went off.

His grandmother now said to him, "It won't be long before you meet up with someone else. We'll see what happens with that one. He'll reveal himself to us in a little while."

After leaving this place, they came upon a mountain of large boulders. This mountain was as huge as Nuvatukya'ovi, but there was no snow on the summit. The boy decided to take a shortcut over the mountain and immediately began to climb. If they went over the crest, they would surely reach the other side. Going around the mountain would mean traveling too great a distance. So the two climbed over the huge boulders.

They were still going along when suddenly there was a noise. The noise caught the boy's attention, so he looked all around the area. The two continued climbing and just as they got to the middle of the mountain, they saw a creature on a ledge above them, pawing the ground with his hoof and snorting all the while. It was a mountain sheep, a very large ram. These sheep lived among the craggy ledges. They looked like the sheep the Hopis kept but were much larger. The one in front of them was a huge ram. No one had ever seen one this big. In addition to his huge size he had a pair of great coiled horns. He did not move from his spot. The two travelers had no choice but to continue upward.

When the boy came up to the ram, it asked, "Hey, who are you that you climbed up here to me without fear? I already know of your winning the race with the deer. That's why you've made it this far. But I doubt you can beat me. I stand on guard here. Look behind you, there's a steep cliff. I won't let anyone through here. Only if you can overcome my power can you continue your journey."

The mountain sheep now stepped up to them. He was clearly more powerful than the deer the youth had first encountered. His horns were very thick and very broad right above his forehead. Also, they had more than one spiral on each side. As he stood there on the ledge pawing the ground with his forefoot, his chest heaved up and down, and he rubbed his horns against the cliff to sharpen them. When the youth was face to face with him, the sheep asked, "You plan to come along here?"

"Yes, I do."

"So I see. Yes, you have passed the deer's post, but now it's time for me to find out about you. I live here, and I rule this whole area. If you are really strong and can conquer me, you're bound to reach your destination."

This is all the ram had to say, so he backed up, stopped, and flung himself toward the boy. Evidently, he meant to crash into the boy and knock him off the ledge. Because this was such a high cliff, the youth would surely die if he fell.

The sheep charged at the boy with great speed. The old woman hastily cried, "Give it all you have. This one is out to trample and kill you. If he gets his horns into you, he'll throw you over the side."

At that moment the boy was standing on a narrow path and had nowhere to flee. It was impossible for him to go backward, for he had just come up over a place with a very steep cliff.

As the ram got closer he lowered his head, preparing to gore the boy. But the boy just stood there with his head darting back and forth. "Dear me, this one will hurt me for sure," he thought as he looked back and forth. Just as the ram closed on him, the boy pressed his back against the side of the cliff. At the same time he reached out and grabbed the ram by the horns, and with all his might broke them off. The ram tumbled to the other side and fell flat. The ram immediately realized that he was lying there without horns. Lifting himself off the ground he said, "Wait! I can't believe it. You're very strong."

The boy now ordered the ram, "Don't come near me. Stay where you are. You'll be hornless now. Perhaps this is why you put me through this—to lose your horns. Even though you may need your horns, I won't return them to you. I was not bothering you, yet you tried to do away with me. So I won't give your horns back to you."

The horns, of course, were the ram's weapons. It was with these that he could kill and he did not want to give them up. So the boy said, "I suppose this is what's on your mind. You're thinking of hurting someone. It would be all right if someone were bothering you but that's not the case. So I will not hand your horns over to you."

"Yes, I do want to keep my horns. I would like to hold on to them because they are my weapons. Give them back. From now on I won't harm anyone with them. What you said is very true. You were not bothering me, and I put you through this test. But that is my reason for being here. I keep an eye on the route that leads to the home of the one whom you seek. He doesn't want me to let just anyone through here. That's why I did this. But I have another pair of horns you may take along with you to Hopiland so that you may benefit from them when the time comes to conduct your ceremony." Then the ram left and soon returned with another pair of horns. From that time on, during the time of the Wuwtsim ceremonial, the members of the Al society donned the horns of the mountain sheep as part of their costume.

In this way the sheep got his horns back and gave the boy another pair in exchange. "Thanks indeed," the boy said. "Thank you so much. I'll be sure to relay your message."

After these words the boy continued on his quest. Twice now he had been tested, and he would be tested again. The youth thought about this, saying to himself, "I now see the reason for my daily running, for my daily exercises. Yes, they are really going to find out if I am brave or not."

With that the boy moved on. The old woman was still accompanying him and said, "We're coming to one now who is heartless. He feels no pity for anyone. He'll try to find out just how brave you are. So go along and be wary. He'll come upon you without warning. He himself is not very brave, but he acts tough because of his huge size."

Old Spider Woman was still talking to him about this when something began approaching them. It was a powerful beast, kicking at the sand in anger. The boy stared at it. At first it seemed to be wearing some sort of headdress, but evidently those were its antlers, which had many branches. "I wonder who this one might be," the youth thought. He sought an answer from the old woman. "Who is this terrible creature?" he asked.

"It is he who inhabits the forest. He is the leader of those who live in the forests. You Hopi people call him an elk. He's the most evil creature of them all and very aggressive," she warned him.

By now the elk had come upon them. Gee, what a bull he was! "So you're coming through here?" the elk inquired, and asked the boy what he was doing there. So then the boy told the elk the purpose of his journey. "Is that right? Very well," was all the elk said.

"Yes. I've been on this trek for several days now and have yet to meet the being I'm looking for. Could you be the one?" he asked.

"No," the elk replied, "you do not seek me. But if you cross my path successfully, you'll find the one you're seeking."

The boy was at a loss just how to act, so he stood there restlessly. "This is a pretty frightening fellow. How would I ever be able to conquer him?" he thought to himself. The old woman told him, "When he runs toward you, aim for his legs with your throwing stick." How lucky it was that he happened to have the flat hunting stick tucked in his belt. "Since he will want to gore you," she said, "he will run straight at you at top speed. You must then also run toward him. Just before you meet face to face, come to a quick stop and take your stick out. Because the elk will be running at full speed, he will be unable to stop as fast as you. Due to his size he won't be able to control himself. Quickly step to one side and throw your stick at him." These were the instructions the old woman gave the boy.

Just as she predicted, the elk charged the boy. He in turn ran toward the elk at full speed. As the elk neared him, the boy drew his hunting stick, and after aiming, hurled it at him. The throw was true, and the elk toppled to the ground with broken legs. This was how the boy conquered his foe.

The elk, now out of breath and gasping for air, said to the boy, "Oh, is this how powerful you are? Still, you have one more test to go." Then the elk continued, "You may enter my realm, for you have beaten me. What a lad you are!"

"Yes," the boy answered, "I guess I have gotten the best of you, so I will enter your realm."

The boy crossed the elk's realm and entered an entirely different area. Many medium-sized buttes were scattered in this area, and the boy and his companion traveled among them. Then his grandmother said to him, "One more test remains. Go along cautiously and not too fast. How awful, we've already encountered three obstacles, and they really put us to the test. Let's not move along too swiftly so that you're not tired before you meet your next challenge. At the next point a most terrible thing awaits us," she said. "It will be your fourth and final test."

And so the two traveled on. At some point along the way Spider Woman said to her grandson, "Look, there to the west in a butte. It's not very large, but it's very slick. When the sun hits it just right," she said, "a bright reflection can be seen. That's it, we're about to approach it, so don't make any mistakes."

Soon they reached the foot of the butte. Apparently, nothing ever grew around this butte. The rocky ground was bare. As the boy stared at the butte it seemed to be smothered with grease. "Why would this thing be like that?" he wondered. The butte was in the middle of the road on which he was traveling and it was in his way. He was faced with the problem of getting to the other side. At first glance there seemed to be no choice but to go through it. But the boy studied the butte and found that it was narrow at the base. He figured he would be able to go around it without having to travel too far before reaching the other side. So he began walking to the north side of it. He was still carrying his grandmother on his ear as he rounded the corner of the butte when suddenly he came upon a large mass of rattlesnakes. What a huge number of serpents there were! He made a slight move to the south and attempted to pass by the snakes, but some of them moved to block his path. The snakes lay coiled in his path, their rattles raising a frightful din. He was just about to attempt another move around them when one of the snakes somehow detected this and lunged for him, but missed.

At this point the boy became afraid and decided to turn back. He tried to retrace his steps and go around the northwest side of the butte, but the snakes were there, too.

He turned to his grandmother and asked, "All right, what do I do now?" The old woman did not reply. He asked again, but still she did not answer. Now he really was at a loss. Overcome with fright, the poor thing just stood there. "Perhaps she hopped off somewhere without letting me know," he thought.

Just then his ear began to itch and he scratched it. At that moment he heard his grandmother say, "Oh my, don't scratch me."

The boy replied, "I thought you left because when I asked you a question, you didn't answer."

"Oh dear, it got so hot that I was overcome by the heat. I dozed off and didn't hear you. What do you mean?" she asked.

So he asked her what they should do to get past the snakes. His grandmother replied, "Don't trifle with these creatures, instead go to the middle of the butte. They won't let you pass on the side," she simply said.

Because his grandmother had always warned him of impeding danger, he asked no more questions and moved to the middle of the butte. Once there, he found someone sitting at the base of the formation. He was sure that this person was not there when he first came up to the butte. All he could see was the person's smooth, round head sticking out of the ground. This person looked up at the boy. What a monstrous being he was! He was a hideous creature whose tongue was flicking in and out at the boy. He didn't know how to go about handling this beast.

Now the old lady gave him more instructions, "Here we must do our utmost. You must give it everything you have."

"I understand," he said, "I'll give it a try. I'll take my chances and approach him. I don't know what he'll do to me, but if luck is with me, he won't harm me and we'll get through to the other side."

Here, for the first time, the boy opened his pouch of cornmeal and took out a small handful. Then he prayed. "If I happen to be lucky, my task won't be difficult," he said in his prayer. He then placed some cornmeal on the ground and approached the being.

How dreadful and ugly he was! "Are you on your way through here, stranger? he asked.

"Yes," the boy replied.

"Very well. Yes, this is the right road," he said. "You cannot get through anywhere else but here. And if you're not afraid of me, come here," he dared the boy.

"Yes, because I'm following instructions, I've put aside my safety and come this far. It seems I'll have to take this road in order to get to my destination. More than once along this road I came face to face with trouble, but still I managed to come this far," he said.

"Yes, this road leads to the destination you seek. And if you're brave enough to enter my home and escape, then you'll have beaten me. You can give it a try at least."

At this moment the boy's grandmother said, "This one is terrible. He knows no mercy. He lives here while he's on duty. No one has ever gotten past him. Many tried in various ways, but not once did anyone succeed or get the best of him. So let's give it our all. Together we're bound to get through here somehow. Just don't be scared. Don't despair."

Relying on each other's strengths, the boy and his grandmother approached the creature. Only Old Spider Woman was unafraid. Now the thing reared up from the ground. Its head was as large as a big water vessel. What the two travelers now saw before them was a huge rattlesnake, so round and smooth that the light reflected off it. He was the being residing at this location. The other snakes around him were his nephews. Together they were standing on guard here.

The old woman said to the boy, "As soon as he confronts you, he'll try to whip his tail around and strike you a big blow with it. The instant his tail comes and is about to strike you, I'll know of this and I will tell you to duck your head."

Thus the two neared the snake. As they went by, the creature raised itself off the ground to a great height, waiting for the boy to make his move. Truly, this was a huge creature. As the boy stepped up to it, the old lady shouted at him from within his ear, "Quick, stoop down!" The boy was on his toes and did as he was told. Just as the old woman had said, the beast whipped its tail around with great speed, narrowly missing the boy's head. The force of the missed blow caused the snake to spin like a top. While the serpent was still spinning, the Old Spider Woman yelled at the boy, "Go on, run."

The boy ran past the snake as fast as he could. The other rattlers were watching their whirling uncle, and before they realized what was happening, the boy had dashed past them. It was only after the youth had reached the other side that the giant serpent calmed down. Beads of sweat were rolling off his body and he had trouble breathing. After getting his breath a little he said, "Hey, you're mighty. You've been the only man to go past my home without any harm. None of those reaching this place has ever survived. Most of them didn't even come this far, for they were killed by the others before they got here. You just did what no one has ever done before. Your bravery has seen you through this test. All right," he continued, "since you have conquered me, you've earned the right to live. It's not too far to the person you seek, and so you'll be able to find him." The serpent still eyed the boy. From all appearances it seemed that he was still going to harm the boy.

However, his grandmother said to him, "He can't hurt you now, it's over.

This is all there is to this. Because you've won, he can't do any harm to you. Continue with your journey."

Now it was the huge rattlesnake that spoke words of encouragement. "All right, go forth with a happy heart. We put you through all these tests, but by conquering your fear you beat all of us. Your heart and mind are pure. That helped you overcome the powers of those who tested your courage."

Thus spoke the serpent, and then he laid out a path of cornmeal for the boy to follow. It was surprising to the boy that the snake knew about such things as a cornmeal path. Once more, the boy and his grandmother set out on their journey. The young man was very happy and said, "Thank you so much. Thanks for laying out this path for me."

"Yes, now go toward your goal with a happy heart. It's not far anymore. You're bound to get there."

In passing through all the realms of those who were guarding this route, the boy had met great difficulties and endured many hardships, but at long last he reached the home of the one who was able to produce warmth.

As the two neared the home, the boy heard that something nearby was making strange noises. Also, he noticed that the air was becoming increasingly warm. The boy had an idea who this person might be. The sounds he heard were similar to those produced by a rattlesnake. Because of this he thought, "Perhaps it's another serpent." Timidly he approached the place from which the noise was coming. He knew, of course, that rattlesnakes are usually out during warm weather. So that is what he thought was making the noise.

The old woman, knowing the boy's fear, said to him, "This one sounds like a rattler but it's not too bad."

Relieved, the boy proceeded. At first he had been walking at a quick pace, but then he slowed down. He almost come to a halt, but upon his grandmother's bidding, he continued.

Once more the two pressed on. It was not long before they again heard the same sizzling noise, but just as quickly it stopped. They listened closely for the sound, but it failed to start up again. The old woman now told him, "We won't find him right away. And even when we come close to him and are standing right above him, we won't be able to spot him. He's going to toy with us for a while, then reveal himself to us," she said. "He isn't the bashful type, but it's never certain where he is. One never knows where his chirping is coming from. But you're bound to find him. He used to live in your homeland." Again the creature resumed its fluting. "That's the only creature that produces a sound like that," the old woman continued. "It is true that once he inhabited the Hopi country, but for some reason he moved here. When he chirps, its impossible to tell where the chirping comes from. Even when you listen closely for him, it sounds like he's right in back of you or next to you." Once more the creature began chirping, and this time he did not stop. The sound seemed to be coming from an area immediately next to them, so they searched for its source. "We haven't come close to it yet," the old woman said.

As they continued their search, they came to a salt bush. That's where the chirping sound seemed to be coming from. The instant the boy came close to the bush, the being became aware of his presence and slipped into his home and enclosed himself inside it. The youth looked all over the shrub but found no trace of the creature. The boy had been standing over the bush for quite some time when the old woman exclaimed, "This is the spot, right here!"

As the two neared the creature's home, the noise grew louder. Once again they began their search but could not find him, despite the fact that they were right at his doorstep. Before long a voice cried, "Here I am!" It seemed as if a lot of voices were speaking at once, but as it turned out there was only one creature there.

The boy and his grandmother inspected the spot, but there didn't seem to be anyone. A little while later they looked below them and, lo and behold, found a man sitting there. He was dressed in rich clothes, and about his neck hung several strands of beads consisting of large nuggets of the finest turquoise. No doubt, this was Cicada. He was the one the youth had sought, and at long last he had found him. Cicada's hair was neatly fixed in a knot, so he looked very handsome. Unfortunately, such a tremendous wave of heat was emanating from his home that it was almost impossible for the boy and his grandmother to approach it.

"This is the way I live; come on in," he said. The boy and his grandmother did as bidden and entered Cicada's home.

The old woman had previously warned the boy, "I won't reveal my presence. They do not know me. That's why I came along with you."

Upon entering Cicada's home, the boy was given a real welcome. Next Cicada prepared a meal for the youth. The boy, in turn, opened his wrapped journey food and invited Cicada to eat. "Here, you eat, too. I didn't finish all of my journey food, so help yourself to what remains."

Cicada heartily ate of the boy's baked sweet cornmeal cakes. "How delicious, how sweet!" he kept saying while he ate. "I've never tasted anything like this before," he said, thanking the boy. He really gorged himself. When he was full, Cicada took a handful of tobacco from his pouch. Since the tobacco leaves were still quite large, he thoroughly crushed them. Next he filled his pipe with them, lit it, and handed it to the youth. The boy took several puffs from the pipe, then returned it. In this way they each gave the other a chance to smoke.

Then Cicada said to the boy, "I'm the one you seek. This is where I make my home."

"Yes, my people sent me on this journey and I've come this far in search of you. I had no idea where I was going while making this trek, but amazingly I arrived right at your place," the boy said.

"Yes, I know what the situation is like out on Hopiland. I know why you are about," Cicada told him.

The boy said, "We plant our seeds during the season when the weather gets warm like this. For this reason the wise elders asked me to seek you out. I forgot about my own safety and did as I was bidden. Your kind, those who know how to produce heat, used to visit our land, but none of you come any more, so the weather is no longer warm."

"Yes, that's right, I live here this far away now. A great many of us live here. All my relatives live here with me, my nephews and nieces, my children, and my grandchildren. Your people are now performing the Soyal ceremony. Two days from now you will begin. Once in a while one of you should make some offerings for me. But you Hopis are beginning to forget about us, and only very rarely will one of your people produce prayer feathers and prayer sticks for us. That's not enough for all of us to pass around and share," he said. "It's these prayer items that we really want from you. But when it comes to Soyalangw, and when you make prayer sticks, you tend to forget us. For this reason my people here seem not very willing any more to visit your country," he said. "So the warmth of the earth does not remain for long. We're the only beings capable of producing heat, yet you treat us with such neglect. You must return to your home and explain to your people what I just told you. When the time for Soyalangw comes, do not forget us—make something for us. Also when you conduct your ceremonies during the summer, make prayer sticks and prayer feathers for us and keep us in mind as you deposit them. As soon as we receive your gifts, we'll help you by producing the warmth necessary for your crops." Now, finally, the boy realized why the cicadas had failed to come to the lands of the Hopi. As he thought it over, it was certainly true that they were no longer chirping at home when it got summer.

Cicada continued, "When the time of Soyalangw approaches, we look forward to it. We wonder how many of your people will make things for us. But unfortunately only one or two do so if they happen to remember us. That's what hurt us and that's why we don't visit your country any more. This you must stress to your people, not to forget us. If they want warmth from us, tell them not to forsake us. We are the only beings who know how to produce heat." To these instructions Cicada added, "I'm going to teach you a song. Upon your return you will teach it to your people so that when you conduct one of your rituals you will include this song in the chants that accompany your prayers." Cicada was now referring to the members of the Flute society. The boy himself belonged to the Flute clan. Cicada was aware of this, so he taught him the song. And he instructed him, "If you sing my song during Soyalangw, you will provide heat for the summer. So remember my song. Your father is the village headman. He'll be able to learn this song." Once more he sang the song to the boy. Four times he repeated it, by then the youth had it memorized. "Have you got it?" Cicada asked.

"Yes, I know the song now."

"Very well," he acknowledged, "don't forget it. All of you must remember it. It is a difficult song, but the one who has a good memory will learn it by heart. Your people eagerly await your return. They're worrying already because you haven't returned. But wait until early tomorrow before you set out."

After this long speech by Cicada the boy unwrapped the mantle that was slung over his shoulders. Then he said to Cicada, "I knew it, there was a reason for you not visiting our country any more. These things my elders made for you before they sent me on this journey. So I brought this along for all of you." The boy then presented the many prayer sticks and prayer feathers to Cicada.

Cicada, upon receiving the gifts from the boy, was overwhelmed with joy. "Thank you very much, this is the way it should be. Thanks for bringing these with you. This very night I'll distribute them among my people. These gifts will gladden their hearts and I'm sure they'll return to your land," he said, gratefully accepting them on behalf of the rest.

The following morning, after feeding the boy and packing food for him, Cicada laid out a cornmeal path for him to follow. Then the boy began his trek homeward. On his way he said to himself, "Oh, such a long distance I have traveled. I guess I'll see many more mornings before I get home. What a long way! On the other hand, I may never get home." He remembered the creatures who had put him through his many ordeals. "They may want to test my courage again." Such troubling thoughts entered his mind as he continued on his way.

At this point his grandmother spoke to him again. "Don't worry, and quicken your pace. Tomorrow they will begin the Soyal ceremony, and we'll arrive just in time."

"But it's still a long ways home from here. We can't get there by tomorrow, even if nothing were to bother me. And even if I run all the way, it'll be a while before I get back," he insisted.

"We'll get there in no time," the old woman assured him. She obviously had something in mind when she said this to the boy. After all, she was a crafty old woman. Then she said to her grandson, "I'm going to shrink the land here. After that we'll be able to go a long distance in a short period of time. The people await your return."

With that she ordered the boy to put her on the ground. Obediently he put her down. Once upon the ground she said, "Close your eyes tight. And not before I tell you can you open them again." The boy did as he was bidden. The old lady now raised up her dress and stuck her buttocks straight up into the air. Next she strained and a large bundle of cobwebs came forth from her anus. This bundle she picked up and wrapped around her hand, making a loop at the end. Then she flung it in the direction of the Hopi country. The cobweb loop caught on something and the old woman began tugging and pulling it back toward her. Lo and behold, along with the cobweb she was dragging a piece of the earth. After she had retrieved the entire piece of cobweb, she said to her grandchild, "Now, with your eyes still closed, take two paces following me." This the boy did. Halting here the old woman repeated the feat. Once again she bade the boy to take two steps, and then the two moved forward.

By the third time she had done this, they had arrived in the vicinity of Nuvatukya'ovi. After the fourth time the two had arrived at the boy's village.

The old woman now said to the boy, "All right, from here on you can go alone. I'll leave you now. I'm glad you were so brave. It was because of this that no harm came to you. You found the person you sought and now are near your home."

The boy thanked the old woman for her help in carrying out his elders' wishes. Then he gave her one of the prayer feathers he had not left with Cicada. "I wish to please you in this small way, so here is one I did not give to Cicada," he told her.

"Thanks so much! I really did not seek anything in return for helping you. But I'm glad you kept this one as a gift for me. That makes me happy. All of you are my grandchildren. I felt sorry for you when I saw your predicament. That's why I came to your aid. Cicada relented and showed his kindness to you. So now you can go back to living as before. Do as he asks and tell your people his whole conversation with you. And now, with a happy heart, go to those who are awaiting you."

"Very well, thank you," the boy said. No sooner had he spoken his last word than Old Spider Woman disappeared. So the boy headed back to the village.

Sure enough, upon entering the village, he noticed that the men were busy preparing prayer sticks in their kivas. Some of the men saw the boy coming and at once were telling each other the news. Since they were anxious to learn the outcome of his trip, they gathered at his home in large numbers. What kind of message would he have for them? The boy told everything about his journey and his accomplishments. When he was alone with his father, he taught him the song from Cicada. So then at Soyalangw, the heads of the village and the members of the Flute clan sang this song in their chants, and it is still used to this day. Every time they performed their ritual, they prayed along with this song. And when it came time for Soyalangw, they made prayer feathers and prayer sticks for the cicadas.

From that point on the lives of the people changed for the better again. The cicadas returned, bringing warmth with them. Once more the weather grew warm when summer came. And when the Hopis sowed their seeds, their crops grew in abundance and matured completely. What a bountiful harvest they reaped! They harvested many things such as corn, beans, squash, watermelon, muskmelon, and other crops.

This was how the boy, with Old Spider Woman's help, was able to locate the cicadas without any harm and bring them back to the Hopi country. And here the story ends.

Figure 12: Fluteplayer images on ceramics

Fluteplayer images are found as decorative motifs on prehistoric pottery (a–k, m, n), and as effigy figures forming the entire vessel (l). The earliest depictions, based on dated pottery types, stem from ca. A.D. 800 (f, g), with the latest occurring between A.D. 1300 to 1600 (c, h). An interesting, but as yet unexplained phenomenon is the existence of fluteplayer images on Hohokam ceramics from the Salt and Gila River drainages in southern Arizona (g, n), in the face of an almost complete absence of such images in the rock art of the same culture area (see Figure 1).

g

h

e

j

k

l

m

n

Conclusion

The impetus for this study lay in two observations. One concerned the increasing popularity of the image of a humpbacked fluteplayer based on rock art depictions, an image called "Kokopelli" after the name of a Hopi kachina. This image is used in a wide variety of contexts and for many unrelated purposes. It is safe to assume that the prehistoric rock art image had a clearly defined and slowly evolving range of meanings and functions in the period when it was created and used, although we have no ethnographic knowledge of their precise nature. The cultural figure bearing the original form of the name affixed to the image is equally traditional but still a living and relevant part of modern Hopi culture, in the form of the Kookopölö kachina. The meaning of the modern forms of the fluteplayer image, however, is not traditional and is quite unstable. Indeed, Kokopelli is associated with a wide variety of functions and characteristics.

The other observation was that the image of the fluteplayer and its modern derivations are not only named after Kookopölö the kachina but to some extent are actually identified with him. However, although the traditional cultural functions of Kookopölö can be named and described, it is at best an open question whether anyone associating Kookopölö with Kokopelli is even aware of these functions.

My intention in this study was to present material and analyses identifying the elements behind the current uses of the Kokopelli image and clear up the confusion between Kokopelli and Kookopölö.

First, there is the fluteplayer image, so common and widespread in prehistoric rock art. The fluteplayer rock art motif originated in the Four Corners area around A.D. 800, reached its zenith from 1100 to 1400, and died out by 1600. As a result of its widespread use, distinctive regional variations developed. The demise of the fluteplayer image was a natural cultural occurrence that took place prior to substantial contact between its Native American creators and the intrusive Anglo culture.

Second, there is the image of a fluteplayer in contemporary popular culture—based on this rock art imagery—that is sometimes insect-like, plays a flute, often has a hump, occasionally displays an erect penis, is credited with a wide variety of characteristics and roles, and carries the name "Kokopelli," derived from the Hopi kachina Kookopölö.

Third, there is the actual Hopi kachina Kookopölö, who always has a hump and traditionally displayed an erect penis intended to illustrate the desirability of human fertility, but who never even carries, much less plays, a flute. He is modeled on an insect, the assassin or robber fly, which has a very pronounced hump. These insects also have a snout from which runs a white stripe, features that are depicted on the mask of the kachina. The association of Kookopölö's mouth protrusion with the flute of the rock art figure, however, is unfounded. The fact that kachina dolls are now being carved that show the god holding a flute is simply a good illustration that the process of acculturation has come full circle.

Hopis view the robber flies as regularly copulating when they meet, and they were once prayed to by Hopi women in the hope of reversing the condition of barrenness. Similarly, Kookopölö is a phallic deity, in that before the influence of the dominant white society, he always appeared ithyphallically. This overt sexual display must be seen as a gesture of deep symbolic significance, an affirmation of the need to generate human life, thereby assuring the very existence and survival of the Hopi people. He is also believed to be an industrious and productive farmer, a trait that is in line with the general aura of fertility and fecundity that surrounds him. Probably related to this is the fact that Kookopölö's hump contains food, seeds, and other good things.

Finally, older Hopis, when confronted with the fluteplayer in rock art, insist on calling him *maahu*, "the cicada," not "Kokopelli." The cicada (confused by many with the locust) in Hopi culture is considered to be "fluting" when it makes its noise, thereby causing *mumkiw*, the gradual heating process that ripens crops. Of all the insects and similar animals that are culturally significant to the Hopi people, the cicada is probably second only to the spider, in the person of Old Spider Woman. The fact that the cicada is one of only five insects that have achieved divine status as a kachina is no doubt due to its ability to make the earth warm.

The cicada is believed to be the owner of a flute, since to the Hopi ear, the sound of the singing insect is reminiscent of that emanating from a *leena*, "flute," the Hopis' only wind instrument. The distinct proboscis of the insect may have reinforced this idea. The cicada is considered the "pet," that is, the patron or totem of the two Hopi flute societies and figures prominently in their rites. The Cicada kachina, however, carries no flute, and unlike Kookopölö, is not humpbacked.

The ethnographic and linguistic material I have been able to collect, including the oral tales, presents insights into traditional Hopi culture as it has survived into our own period, even though many of its features may now be disappearing. This material also provides proof that the rock art fluteplayer more closely resembles the cicada in Hopi culture than it does Kookopölö.

Cultural development has its disruptions and discontinuities, and all cultures incorporate material from alien sources. We have to grant the prehistoric American Indian cultures of the Southwest that used this image and the historic culture of the Hopi just as much capacity for change as we grant our own dominant culture. Although we assume that they were more stable and developed more slowly than what can be observed today, both the figure of the fluteplayer and that of the kachina may have undergone significant changes not only in appearance and appellation but also in cultural function.

The popular Western assumption that "the Indians" from prehistoric times to the present are characterized by cultural sameness and stability, by a holistic and monolithic cultural system, an assumption that seems to have contributed to the popularity of the Kokopelli variant of the fluteplayer, is absurd and constitutes an ethnic stereotype. While the preservation of cultural knowledge is just as important as that of endangered species, it should not lead to putting traditional tribal cultures into an intellectual museum as live artifacts. Where I point out the unauthentic aspects of the Kokopelli phenomenon, it is done with an awareness that even an interpretive concept of cultural description such as Geertz's "thick description" (1973: 3–30), which endeavors to see culture as a network or web of meanings into which humanity is woven, will inadequately describe the dynamics of every culture.

Cultures are open systems subject not only to internal innovation but also in particular to changes effected by contact with others. In the words of Clifford (1988: 14), "cultural difference is no longer a stable, exotic otherness, self-other relations are matters of power and rhetoric rather than of essence. A whole structure of expectations about authenticity in culture and art is thrown in doubt." Ironically, one of the unauthentic aspects of Kokopelli is that which endows the image with notions of a timeless authenticity.

In the Kokopelli phenomenon we have a genuine case of cultural hybridity, or what might be called "bilateral acculturation." On the one hand, Anglo popular culture has accepted the figure, though not without first making it "safe" by eliminating the erect phallus in most representations. Although there is no specific evidence, archaeologists believe that the prehistoric flute-player was primarily a religious icon. The Kokopelli image of today, however, has become primarily secular, despite its association with the deity Kookopölö in Hopi ritual. Some members of Hopi culture, on the other hand, apparently have accepted the figure with a flute, possibly by bowing to Anglo market demands or by being unaware that such a Kookopölö representation does not occur in traditional Hopi culture.

We may deplore this situation. Still, intercultural borrowings, especially where there is economic or political pressure or incentive, are normal occurrences and not to be labeled either positive or negative. We have no right to demand that "traditional" cultures remain unchanged for our benefit. And while we may criticize the Kokopelli craze as being the result of cultural exploitation by the dominant culture, in this postcolonial age we could just as easily see it as a change in the dominant culture through counteracculturation by Native Americans.

It is apparent that the Kokopelli phenomenon arose in the late twentieth century and continues to grow because it fulfills a number of psychological needs, such as that for mystery and wildness in what many see as an increasingly sterile and impersonal world. It is part of a Western exoticism that has always included aspects of cultural self-criticism by pointing to deficits of meaning, order, and values in Western society. The semantically and functionally uncertain qualities of the Kokopelli image turn it into a kind of cultural wild card, a joker that can be used to fill a variety of positions. Its associations with music, its lyrical "Italian-sounding" name, its aesthetic appeal, its non-threatening appearance, and its connection with fertility (for those with enough background knowledge to be aware of that aspect), all contribute to turning it into a commodity in keeping with the multiethnic cultural economy of the American Southwest. At the same time, these associations create an intercultural wanderer, revealing not only the derivativeness and the lack of taste and cultural respect in our world but also the innovative potential inherent in any meeting of cultures.

Appendix: The Hopi Alphabet

Hopi, an American Indian language spoken in northeastern Arizona, is a branch of the large Uto-Aztecan family of languages that covers vast portions of the western United States and Mexico. It is related to such languages as Tohono O'odham, Southern Paiute, Shoshone, Tarahumara, Yaqui, and Nahuatl, the language of the Aztecs, to mention only a few. Navajo, Apache, Havasupai, Zuni, Tewa, and many other languages in the American Southwest are completely unrelated to it, however. At least three regional Hopi dialects, whose differences in terms of pronunciation, grammar, and vocabulary are relatively minimal, can be distinguished. No prestige dialect exists.

While traditionally the Hopi, like most American Indian groups, never developed a writing system of their own, there today exists a standardized—yet unofficial—orthography for the Hopi language. Ronald W. Langacker has presented a "simple and linguistically sound writing system" (Milo Kalectaca, *Lessons in Hopi*, edited by Ronald W. Langacker [Tucson: University of Arizona Press, 1978]) for the Second Mesa dialect of Shungopavi (Songoopavi). My own generalized Hopi orthography is equally phonemic in nature and is based on the dialect habits of speakers from the Third Mesa communities of Hotevilla (Hotvela), Bacavi (Paaqavi), Oraibi (Orayvi), Kykotsmovi (Kiqötsmovi), and Moencopi (Munqapi), who comprise the majority of Hopis. Speakers from the First Mesa villages of Walpi and Sichomovi (Sitsom'ovi) as well as from the communities of Shungopavi (Songoopavi), Mishongnovi (Musangnuvi), and Shipaulovi (Supawlavi) simply need to impose their idiosyncratic pronunciation on the written "image" of the preponderant dialect, much as some speakers in the northeastern United States would interpret the spelling of "car" as [ca:], whereas most other Americans pronounce it as [car].

Hopi standardized orthography is thus truly pan-Hopi; it is characterized by a close fit between phonemically functional sound and corresponding symbol. Unusual graphemes are avoided. For example, the digraph *ng* stands for the same phoneme that *ng* represents in English si*ng*. Symbols like *ñ*, as the translator of the New Testament into Hopi elected to do, or *ŋ*, which is suggested in the symbol inventory of the International Phonetic Alphabet, are not employed. In all, twenty-one letters are sufficient to write Hopi, of which only the umlauted *ö* is not part of the English alphabet. For the glottal stop, one of the Hopi consonants, the apostrophe is used.

Hopi distinguishes the six vowels *a, e, i, o, ö,* and *u,* the last of which represents the international phonetic symbol *ɨ*. Their long counterparts are written by doubling the letter for the corresponding short vowel: *aa, ee, ii, oo, öö,* and *uu.* The short vowels are found in combination with both the *y-* and *w-* glide to form the following diphthongs: *ay, ey, iy, oy, öy, uy,* and *aw, ew, iw, öw, uw.* Only the diphthong *ow* does not occur. The inventory of consonants contains a number of sounds which have to be represented as digraphs or trigraphs (two- or three-letter combinations): *p, t, ky, k, kw, q, qw, ', 'y, m, n, ngy, ng, ngw, ts, v, r, s,* and *l.* The two semi-vowels are the glides *w* and *y.* Notably absent are the sounds *b, d,* and *g,* to mention only one prominent difference between the Hopi and English sound inventories. Because Hopi *p, t,* and *k* are pronounced without aspiration, speakers of English tend to hear them as *b, d,* and *g.* This accounts for many wrong spellings of Hopi words in the past.

The following table lists all the functional Hopi sounds, with the exception of those characterized by a falling tone—a phonetic feature not shared by First and Second Mesa speakers. Each phoneme is illustrated by a Hopi example and accompanied by phonetic approximations drawn from various European languages.

Phoneme	Sample Word		Sound Approximations		
			English (E), French (F) German (G), Spanish (S)		
1. Vowels:					
(a) short vowels					
a	p*a*s	very	E p*o*t	S *ca*s*a*	
e	p*e*p	there	E m*e*t	F p*è*re	
i	s*i*hu	flower	E h*i*t	G m*i*t	
o	m*o*mi	forward	E *o*bey	F c*o*l	G s*o*ll
ö	q*ö*tö	head	F n*eu*f	G L*ö*ffel	

u	t*u*wa	he found it	similar to E g*oo*d but with lips very much spread	

(b) long vowels

aa	p*aa*s	carefully	E p*a*lm	G St*aa*t
ee	p*ee*p	almost	same as *e* in E l*e*t but drawn out F *ê*tre	G M*äh*ne
ii	s*ii*hu	intestines	E l*ea*ky but drawn out and without diphthongization F r*i*re	G w*ie*
oo	m*oo*mi	he is pigeon-toed	similar to E l*o*w but without the diphthongization at the end F r*o*se	G B*oo*t
öö	q*öö*tö	suds	F f*eu*	G T*ö*ne
uu	t*uu*wa	sand	same as Hopi *u* but drawn out	

2. Diphthongs:
(a) with y-glide

ay	ts*ay*	small/young	E fl*y*	G Kl*ei*der
ey	*ey*kita	he groans	E m*ay*	
iy	yaap*iy*	from here on	E fl*ea* + E *y*es	
oy	ah*oy*	back to	E t*oy*	G h*eu*te
öy	h*öy*kita	he growls	F *oei*l	
uy	*uy*to	he goes planting	Hopi *u* + E *y*es G pf*ui* but with lips spread instead of rounded	

(b) with w-glide

aw	*aw*ta	bow	E f*ow*l	G M*au*s
ew	p*ew*	here (to me)	E m*e*t + E *w*et	
iw	p*iw*	again	E h*i*t + E *w*et	

ow	nonexisting		
öw	ngöl*öw*ta	it is crooked	G Löffel + E *w*et
uw	p*uw*moki	he got sleepy	Hopi *u* + E *w*et

3. Consonants:
(a) stops

p	*p*aahu	water/spring	F *p*ain	E s*p*it (without aspiration as in *p*it)
t	*t*upko	younger brother	F *t*able	E *t*oy but without aspiration
ky	*ky*aaro	parrot	E *c*ure but without aspiration	
k	*k*oho	wood/stick	F *c*ar	E s*k*y (without aspiration as in *c*at)
kw	*kw*ala	it boiled	E *qu*it but without aspiration	
q	*q*ööha	he built a fire	like E *c*ool but articulated further back in mouth; tongue at back of soft palate	
qw	yang*qw*	from here	E *w*et, added to pronunciation of *q*	
'	pu'	now/today	E oh-'oh	G Ver'ein
'y	ki'*y*ta	he has a house	glottal stop followed by a very brief [i]-sound	

(b) nasals

m	*m*alatsi	finger	E *m*e	
n	*n*aama	both/together	E *n*ut	
ngy	*ngy*am	clan members	E ki*ng* + E *y*es	
ng	*ng*öla	wheel	E ki*ng*	G fa*ng*en
ngw	kooya*ngw*	spider	E ki*ng* + E *w*et	

(c) affricate

ts	*ts*uku	point/clown	E hi*ts*	G Zunge

(d) fricatives

v	*v*otoona	coin/button	E *v*eal	G *W*inter
r	*r*oya	it turned	syllable initial position: E lei*s*ure (with tongue tip curled toward palate)	
r	hin'u*r*	very (female speaking)	syllable final position: E *sh*ip	F *ch*arme
s	*s*akuna	squirrel	E *s*ong	
h	*h*o'apu	carrying basket	E *h*elp	

(e) lateral

l	*l*aho	bucket	E *l*ot

4. Glides:
(a) preceding a vowel

w	*w*aala	gap/notch	E *w*et
y	*y*uutu	they ran	E *y*es

(b) succeeding a vowel
see diphthongs

   Hopi word stress in two-syllable words is generally on the first syllable. Longer words are also accented on the second syllable unless the first syllable is long. The latter is considered long if its vowel is followed by two consonants, or if it contains either a long vowel or diphthong. Such words with long first syllables receive the primary stress on the initial syllable.

   Exceptions to these rules would normally be marked with an acute accent on the vowel of the stressed syllable. However, since Second Mesa speakers, in some cases, follow stress rules differing from those applicable for Third Mesa speakers, exceptions are not marked in the narratives here. Nor is falling tone indicated in them, since this phenomenon as absent from the dialects spoken by non-Third Mesa speech communities.

Bibliography

Alpert, Joyce M.
    1991   "Kokopelli: A New Look at the Humpbacked Flute Player in
            Anasazi Rock Art." *American Indian Art Magazine* 17(1):48–57.

Anati, Emmanuel
    1993   *World Rock Art: The Primordial Language*. Vol. 12. Studi Camuni,
            Edizioni del Centro. Capo de Ponte: Centro Camuno di Studi
            Prehistorici.

Anderson, Bruce
    1976   "Kokopelli: The Humpbacked Flute Player." *American Indian Art
            Magazine* 1(2):36–40.

Aron, Fanchon
    1981   "Kokopelli: Petroglyphs on the Pajarito Plateau." *El Palacio* 87
            (2):13–15.

Bartman, Nancy
    1979   "The Humpbacked Flute Player in Anasazi Rock Art: An Icono-
            graphic Analysis." Senior thesis, Department of Anthropology,
            University of Pennsylvania.

Beaglehole, Ernest
    1937   "Notes on Hopi Economic Life." *Yale University Publications in
            Anthropology* 15:1–59.

Bradfield, Richard Maitland
    1973   *A Natural History of Associations: A Study in the Meaning of Commu-
            nity*. Vol. 2. New York: International Universities Press.

Brill, Lois
    1984   "Kokopelli: An Analysis of his Alleged Attributes and Suggestions
            Toward Alternate Identifications." Master's thesis, Department of
            Art, University of New Mexico.

Bruggmann, Maximilien, and Sylvio Acatos
    1990   *Pueblos: Prehistoric Indian Cultures of the Southwest.* New York: Facts on File.

Caduto, Michael J., and Joseph Bruchac
    1988   *Keepers of the Earth: Native American Stories and Environmental Activities for Children.* Golden, CO: Fulcrum.

Capinera, John L.
    1995   "Humpbacked Flute Player and Other Entomomorphs from the American Southwest." *American Entomologist* 41(2):83–88.

Carr, Pat
    1979   "Mimbres Mythology." *Southwestern Studies*, Monograph no. 56. El Paso: Texas Western Press.

Cawley, John
    1966   "The Humpback Flute Player Kokopelli." *The Bulletin* (Kern County Medical Society) 13(5):168–69, 285.

    1974   "The Hump-back Controversy." *La Pintura* 1(1):3–4.

Clifford, James
    1988   *The Predicament of Culture: Twentieth-Century Ethnography, Literature, and Art.* Cambridge, MA: Harvard University Press.

Colton, Harold S.
    1949   *Hopi Kachina Dolls with a Key to Their Identification.* Albuquerque: University of New Mexico Press.

    1970   *Hopi Kachina Dolls with a Key to Their Identification.* 2d rev. ed. Albuquerque: University of New Mexico Press.

Conway, Thor
    1993   *Painted Dreams.* Minocqua, WI: NorthWord Press.

Cushing, Frank Hamilton
    1923   "Origin Myth from Oraibi." *Journal of American Folk-Lore* 36:163–70.

Cutler, Hugh C.

1944   "Medicine Men and the Preservation of a Relict Gene in Maize."
Journal of Heredity 35:290–94.

Davis, John V.

1975   Letter to *La Pintura* 1(4): 7.

Dockstader, Frederick J.

1954   *The Kachina and the White Man.* Bulletin 35. Bloomfield Hills, MI:
Cranbrook Institute of Science.

Erickson, Jon T.

1977   *Kachinas: An Evolving Hopi Art Form?* Phoenix: Heard Museum.

Fewkes, Jesse Walter

1894   "The Walpi Flute Observance: A Study of Primitive Dramatiza-
tion." *Journal of American Folk-Lore* 7:265–88.

1895   "The Oraibi Flute Altar." *Journal of American Folk-Lore* 8:265–84.

1896   "The Miconinovi Flute Altars." *Journal of American Folk-Lore* 9:241–
56.

1898   "Archaeological Expedition to Arizona in 1895." In *Bureau of
American Ethnology, 17th Annual Report for the Years 1895–1896,*
2:519–742. Washington, D.C.: Smithsonian.

1903   "Hopi Katcinas Drawn by Native Artists." In *Bureau of American
Ethnology, 21st Annual Report for the Years 1899–1901,* 3–126.
Washington, D.C.: Smithsonian.

Fewkes, Jesse Walter, and Alexander Stephen

1892   "The Na-ac-nai-ya: A Tusayan Initiation Ceremony." *Journal of
American Folk-Lore* 5(18):189–221.

Geertz, Armin W.

1984   "A Reed Pierced the Sky: Hopi Indian Cosmography on Third
Mesa, Arizona." *Numen* 31(2):216–41.

1994 *The Invention of Prophecy: Continuity and Meaning in Hopi Indian Religion*. Berkeley: University of California Press.

Geertz, Clifford
1973 "Thick Description: Toward an Interpretive Theory of Culture." In *The Interpretation of Cultures: Selected Essays*, 3–30. New York: Basic Books.

Gill, Sam D.
1987 *Mother Earth: An American Story*. Chicago: University of Chicago Press.

Grant, Campbell
1967 *Rock Art of the American Indian*. New York: Thomas Y. Crowell.

Hartmann, Horst
1978 *Kachina-Figuren der Hopi Indianer*. Berlin: Museum für Völkerkunde.

Hawley, Florence
1937 "Kokopelli of the Prehistoric Southwestern Pueblo Pantheon." *American Anthropologist* 39:644–46.

Hill, Stephen
1995 *Kokopelli Ceremonies*. Santa Fe: Kiva Publishing.

Hillerman, Tony
1988 *A Thief of Time*. New York: Harper and Row.

Hirschmann, Fred, and Scott Thybony
1994 *Rock Art of the American Southwest*. Portland, OR: Graphic Arts Center.

Hunger, Heinz
1977 "Die Heilige Hochzeit: Jagdzauber und Fruchtbarkeitskult." *Sexualmedizin* 1977:667–700.

Hurst, Winston B., and Joe Pachak
1989 *Spirit Windows: Native American Rock Art of Southeastern Utah*. Blanding, UT: n.p.

Jones, Paul A.
   1953   *Blue Feather: A Story of Prehistoric Indian Life Based on a Navajo Legend.* Lyons, KS: Prairie Publishers.

Kabotie, Fred
   1977   *Fred Kabotie: Hopi Indian Artist: An Autobiography Told with Bill Belknapp.* Flagstaff: Museum of Northern Arizona with Northland Press.

Kidder, Alfred V., and Samuel J. Guernsey
   1919   "Archeological Explorations in Northeastern Arizona." Bulletin 65. Washington, DC: Bureau of American Ethnology.

Klausnitzer, Bernhard
   1987   *Insects: Their Biology and Cultural History.* New York: Universe Books.

Knauth, Percy
   1970   *The Illustrated Encyclopedia of the Animal Kingdom.* Vol. 16. New York: Danbury Press.

Lambert, Marjorie F.
   1957   "A Rare Stone Humpbacked Figurine from Pecos Pueblo, New Mexico. *El Palacio* 64:93–108.

   1967   "A Kokopelli Effigy Pitcher from Northwestern New Mexico." *American Antiquity* 32(3):398–401.

Lewis-Williams, J. D.
   1995   "Some Aspects of Rock Art Research in the Politics of Present-Day South Africa." In *Perceiving Rock Art: Social and Political Perspectives,* edited by Knut Helskog and Bjørnar Olsen, 317–37. Oslo: Novus Forlag.

Linsenmaier, Walter
   1972   *Insects of the World.* New York: McGraw-Hill.

Lockett, Hattie G.
1933   *The Unwritten Literature of the Hopi*. University of Arizona Bulletin
        4(4). Social Science Bulletin no. 2. Tucson: University of Arizona.

Lyon, Fern
1995   Review of *Kokopelli: Flute Player Images in Rock Art*, by Dennis Slifer
        and James Duffield, *New Mexico Magazine* 73(11):11.

Mails, Thomas E.
1983   *The Pueblo Children of the Earth Mother*. Garden City, NY: Double-
        day.

Mallery, Garrick
1893   "Picture-Writing of the American Indians." *Tenth Annual Report of
        the Bureau of Ethnology*. Reprint, 1972. New York: Dover.

Malotki, Ekkehart
1983a   *Hopi Time: A Linguistic Analysis of the Temporal Concepts in the Hopi
        Language*. Trends in Linguistics. Studies and Monographs 20.
        Edited by Werner Winter. Berlin: Mouton.

1983b   "The Story of the 'Tsimonmamant' or Jimson Weed Girls: A Hopi
        Narrative Featuring the Motif of the Vagina Dentata." In *Smoothing
        the Ground: Essays on Native American Oral Literature*, edited by
        Brian Swann, 204–20. Berkeley: University of California Press.

1991   "Language as a Key to Cultural Understanding: New Interpre-
        tations of Central Hopi Concepts." *Baessler Archiv* 39(1):43–75.

Malotki, Ekkehart, editor
1993   *Hopi Ruin Legends. Kiqötutuwutsi*. Narrated by Michael
        Lomatuway'ma, Lorena Lomatuway'ma, and Sidney Namingha Jr.
        Lincoln: University of Nebraska Press.

1995   *The Bedbugs' Night Dance and Other Hopi Sexual Tales. Mumuspi'y-
        yungqa Tuutuwutsi*. Narrated by Michael Lomatuway'ma, Lorena
        Lomatuway'ma, Sidney Namingha Jr., Leslie Koyawena, and
        Herschel Talashoma. Lincoln: University of Nebraska Press.

1998   *Hopi Animal Tales*. Narrated by Michael Lomatuway'ma, Lorena Lomatuway'ma, and Sidney Namingha Jr. Lincoln: University of Nebraska Press.

Martineau, LaVan
1973   *The Rocks Begin to Speak*. Las Vegas: KC Publications.

McCreery, Patricia, and Ekkehart Malotki
1994   *Tapamveni: The Rock Art Galleries of Petrified Forest and Beyond*. Petrified Forest, AZ: Petrified Forest Museum Association.

Miller, Jay
1975   "Kokopelli." In *Collected Papers in Honor of Florence Hawley Ellis*, edited by Theodore R. Frisbie, 2:371–80. Norman, OK: Archaeological Society of New Mexico.

Neary, John
1992   "Kokopelli Kitsch." *Archaeology* 45(6):76.

Nequatewa, Edmund
1946   "A Flute Ceremony at Hotevilla." *Plateau* 19(2):35–36.

O'Toole, Christopher, and K. G. Preston-Mafham
1985   *Insects in Camera: A Photographic Essay on Behavior*. Oxford: Oxford University Press.

Parsons, Elsie Clews
1926   "Tewa Tales." Memoirs 19. New York: American Folk-Lore Society.

1938   "The Humpbacked Flute Player of the Southwest." *American Anthropologist* 40:337–38.

1939   *Pueblo Indian Religion*. Chicago: University of Chicago Press.

Patterson-Rudolph, Carol
1990   *Petroglyphs and Pueblo Myths of the Rio Grande*. Albuquerque: Avanyu.

Payne, Richard W. and Eula M.
  1976   "Kokopelli the Flautist." *Oklahoma Today* 26(3):34.

Renaud, Etienne B.
  1938   *Petroglyphs of North Central New Mexico*. Archaeological Survey
           Series, Eleventh Report. Denver: University of Denver Department
           of Anthropology.

  1948   "Kokopelli: A Study in Pueblo Mythology." *Southwestern Lore*
           14:25–40.

Ritter, Dale W., and Eric W. Ritter
  1977   "The Influence of the Religious Formulator in Rock Art of North
           America." In *American Indian Rock Art*, edited by A. J. Bock, Frank
           Bock, and John Cawley, 3:63–79. Whittier, CA: American Rock Art
           Research Association.

Rosenberger, Edythe H.
  1956   "The Flute Ceremony at Mishongnovi—1954." *El Museo* n.s. 2(1):3–
           13.

Russel, Sharman A.
  1991   *Songs of the Fluteplayer: Seasons of Life in the Southwest*. Reading, MA:
           Addison-Wesley.

Salter, John R.
  1960   "A Comparison of Two Fertility Figures." *Monument: A Review of
           the Humanities and the Arts* 1:16–24.

Secakuku, Alph H.
  1995   *Following the Sun and Moon: Hopi Kachina Tradition*. Flagstaff: North-
           land Publishing.

Seymour, Tryntje Van Ness
  1988   *When the Rainbow Touches Down*. Phoenix: The Heard Museum.

Slifer, Dennis, and James Duffield
  1994   *Kokopelli: Flute Player Images in Rock Art*. Santa Fe: Ancient City
           Press.

Smith, Watson

1952   "Kiva Mural Decorations at Awatovi and Kawaika-a." *Papers of the Peabody Museum of Archaeology and Ethnology 37.*

Smithsonian Institution

1979   *The Year of the Hopi: Paintings and Photographs by Joseph Mora, 1904–06.* With essays by Tyrone Stewart, Frederick Dockstader, and Barton Wright. Washington, D.C.: Smithsonian.

Stephen, Alexander M.

1929   "Hopi Tales." *Journal of American Folk-Lore* 42(163):1–72.

1936   *Hopi Journal.* 2 vols. Edited by Elsie Clews Parsons. Columbia University Contributions to Anthropology 3. New York: Columbia University.

Stevenson, Matilda

1915   *Ethnobotany of the Zuni Indians. Thirtieth Annual Report of the Bureau of American Ethnology, 1908–1909.* Reprint, 1993. New York: Dover.

Swan, Lester A., and Charles S. Papp

1972   *The Common Insects of America.* New York: Harper and Row.

Teiwes, Helga

1991   *Kachina Dolls: The Art of Hopi Carvers.* Tucson: University of Arizona Press.

Tisdale, Shelby J.

1993   "From Rock Art to Wal-Mart: Kokopelli Representations in Historical Perspective." *Papers of the Archaeological Society of New Mexico* 19:213–23.

Titiev, Mischa

1937   "A Hopi Salt Expedition." *American Anthropologist* 39(2):244–58.

1938   "Hopi Racing Customs." *Papers of the Michigan Academy of Science, Arts, and Letters* 24(4):33–42.

1939   "The Story of Kokopele." *American Anthropologist* n.s. 41:91–98.

1944   "Old Oraibi: A Study of the Hopi Indians of Third Mesa." *Papers of the Peabody Museum of American Archaeology and Ethnology* 22(1).

1972   *The Hopi Indians of Old Oraibi: Change and Continuity.* Ann Arbor: University of Michigan Press.

Turner, Christy G., II
1963   "Petrographs of the Glen Canyon Region." Bulletin 38. Flagstaff: Museum of Northern Arizona.

Tyler, Hamilton A.
1975   *Pueblo Animals and Myths*. Norman: University of Oklahoma Press.

Vogl, Alfred
1970   "The Kokopelli." *Journal of the American Medical Association* 214 (3):599.

Voth, Henry R.
1905   "The Traditions of the Hopi." *Anthropological Series* 8:1–319. Chicago: Field Columbian Museum.

1912   "Tawa Baholawu of the Oraibi Flute Societies." In "Brief Miscellaneous Hopi Papers," 123–36. *Anthropological Series* 11(2):89–149. Chicago: Field Columbian Museum.

Walker, Dave
1998   *Cuckoo for Kokopelli*. Flagstaff: Northland Publishing.

Washburn, Dorothy K.
1980   *Hopi Kachina: Spirit of Life*. San Francisco: California Academy of Sciences.

Waters, Frank
1963   *Book of the Hopi*. New York: Viking.

Webb, Gerald
1936   *Tuberculosis. Clio Medica* vol. 7. New York: Paul B. Hoebner.

Webb, William, and Robert A. Weinstein

1973   *Dwellers at the Source: Southwestern Indian Photographs of A. C. Vroman, 1895–1904.* New York: Grossman.

Wellmann, Klaus F.

1970   "Kokopelli of Indian Paleology: Hunchbacked Rain Priest, Hunting Magician, and Don Juan of the Old Southwest." *Journal of the American Medical Association* 212(10):1678–82.

1974   "Kokopelli as Southwestern Manifestation of the Universal Trickster Archetype." *La Pintura* 1(2):2, 4, 6.

Whiting, Alfred F.

1966   *Ethnobotany of the Hopi.* Bulletin of the Museum of Northern Arizona 15. Flagstaff: Northland Press.

Widdison, Jerold

1991   *The Anasazi: Why Did They Leave? Where Did They Go?* Albuquerque: Southwest Natural and Cultural Heritage Association.

Wright, Barton

1973   *Hopi Kachinas: A Hopi Artist's Documentary.* Flagstaff: Northland Press.

1977   *Hopi Kachinas: The Complete Guide to Collecting Kachina Dolls.* Flagstaff: Northland Press.

1979   *Hopi Material Culture: Artifacts Gathered by H. R. Voth in the Fred Harvey Collection.* Flagstaff: Northland Press and Heard Museum.

1985   *Kachinas of the Zuni.* Flagstaff: Northland Press.

1993   "The Search for Kokopelli." *Arizona Highways* 69(7):15–17.

1994   *The Clowns of the Hopi.* Flagstaff: Northland Publishing.

Young, John V.

1965   "The Peregrinations of Kokopelli." *Westways* 57(9):39–41.

1990   *Kokopelli: Casanova of the Cliff Dwellers.* Palmer Lake, CO: Filter Press.

Index

Tyler, Hamilton, 71

Utah, southern, 6

Vogl, Alfred, 10
Voth, Henry R., 12, 61, 63, 69, 71

Walker, Dave, 2
Washburn, Dorothy, 33
Waters, Frank, 7, 9–10, 12, 51, 65, 75
Webb, Gerald, 3, 25
Webb, William, 69
Weinstein, Robert, 69
Wellman, Klaus, 7, 10, 25, 43, 51, 57
Whiting, Alfred, 77
Whorf, Benjamin Lee, x
Widdison, Jerold, 39
Willow Springs, 68
Wright, Barton, 10–11, 23–24, 29, 32,
   49, 55–56, 77
wukwtuvoyla (old age marker), 32
wuuti (woman), 51

Xochipilli, 8
Young, John, 9–11
Zuni, 2, 8–9, 11 n. 2, 23, 26, 49, 77, 141